Into The
Promised Land

Beyond the Lesbian Struggle

Jeanette Howard

MONARCH
BOOKS

Oxford, UK & Grand Rapids, Michigan

First published in the UK in 2005 by Monarch Books
(a publishing imprint of Lion Hudson plc),
Mayfield House, 256 Banbury Road, Oxford OX2 7DH
Tel: +44 (0) 1865 302750 Fax: +44 (0) 1865 302757
Email: monarch@lionhudson.com
www.lionhudson.com

Distributed by:
UK: Marston Book Services Ltd, PO Box 269,
Abingdon, Oxon OX14 4YN
USA: Kregel Publications, PO Box 2607,
Grand Rapids, Michigan 49501

ISBN 1 85424 676 3 (UK)
ISBN 0 8254 6076 X (USA)

British Library Cataloguing Data
A catalogue record for this book is available
from the British Library.

Book design and production for the publishers
by Lion Hudson plc
Printed in Great Britain.

Dedication

Into the Promised Land is dedicated to my father, Bob, who died during the writing of this book. As a keen gardener and lover of the natural world, my dad always believed in God the Creator. But only as illness increasingly prevented him from working in the garden did my father gradually become acquainted with his Saviour.

My dad was reconciled to God through our Lord Jesus Christ just before he died, and for that act of divine love and grace I shall be eternally grateful.

This book is dedicated to my earthly father for the praise and glory of my heavenly Father.

Contents

Acknowledgments

It is with immense love and gratitude that I acknowledge my mother, Joan, and my sister, Helena, for their unwavering love and support over the past ten, often difficult, years. I appreciate that they haven't always understood my ways, or me, but they have never failed to "be there" through it all.

Once again, I thank the members of Battle Baptist Church for their friendship and support. There has been the obvious practical help many have offered over recent years, and the unseen and equally valued prayer support that has been undertaken on my behalf. May God bless you all for the love you have shown towards me.

Thanks also go to Alison John and Sonia Balcer who both read the manuscript and offered suggestions, and to Vivien Drakes for her proofreading. Their unrelenting use of a red pen has proved beyond doubt that I was absent from school the day the dreaded apostrophe was taught!

Introduction

No one could ever accuse me of being a prolific writer! It has been thirteen years since *Out of Egypt* was first published, and I am grateful to Tony Collins and those at Monarch Books for their patience ever since.

I have had to live and digest much of *Into the Promised Land* before I could ever put pen to paper. Certainties that I held, back in the late 1980s, regarding sexual "healing" have become less certain and less static in nature. I have walked away from the "either/ors" to what I believe to be a richer understanding of what it means when Paul says, "Work out your salvation with fear and trembling" (Philippians 2:12b).

In addressing my homosexuality over the years, there is much to be grateful for. I have been able to cast off the identity I laboured under as a lesbian, and have truly been able to embrace my identity as a child of God: an equally terrifying and liberating experience! Learning to develop safe boundaries with other women was not without its difficulties, but, over the years, I have learned how to avoid unnecessary temptation and develop valuable friendships, based not on gay attraction but on the genuine love of a sister in Christ. That process is ongoing.

However, the past 18 years of Christian living have not been plain sailing. Along with the joy of knowing Christ and the privilege of teaching his word, I have experienced the pain of deep cyclical depression that has often paralysed my walk as well as my work.

Three years ago, I took stock of my situation. Despite all my efforts, prayer, application and service, I had to admit that I had not travelled along a continuum and entered the world of heterosexuality. Although my identity was not found in lesbianism, and I no longer felt compelled to engage in lesbian sexual behaviour, there appeared to be no further movement. Despite joining a Christian dating agency and opening myself up to many avenues of experience, I could not honestly see myself ever committing to a man. It was time to own the truth.

Living in a conversely hopeful/hopeless land of possible change had left me exhausted, powerless and well short of the promised abundant life (John 10:10). However, accepting that my attractions, if fostered, would lead to a recurrence of lesbian behaviour proved beneficial. An unseen, and largely unknown, barrier between Jesus and me was demolished. Relating to him from the position of who I am, and not who I would like to be, released a greater intimacy between us. Subsequently, a hungry heart finally began to be fed.

So where do I stand today? A number of people claim to have changed in their orientation and behaviour from that of homosexual to heterosexual. Others claim to be well advanced in that change process. I do not intend to challenge such statements. Only an individual can know his or her own true condition.

There are other women who, like me, have tried for many years to throw off lesbian attraction and foster a more heterosexual mindset. We have wanted to be free to marry and start a family, but that freedom has never materialised. For a variety of reasons, many of those women have opted for a monogamous lesbian relationship while still following Christ.

I understand their behaviour, but I cannot agree with it.

People I greatly respect have been mulling over this issue for some time and have shifted 180 degrees in their thinking. Jeremy Marks, director of Courage, a UK-based ministry, is one such person. Initially founded as a ministry to help Christian men and women address and overcome their same-sex attractions, Courage has now shifted its position. Jeremy's conclusion, initially prompted by people's apparent "failure" to change, is summed up in the following statement taken from the Courage website: "From ongoing prayer and bible study, currently my conclusions are that although we must shun the pursuit of "recreational sex", there is scope in scripture for acceptance of godly, intimate same-sex relationships."[1]

Three years since that statement, Jeremy has further clarified his position:

> Throughout scripture, we see that it is our underlying attitudes and motivation that are the determining factors as to whether or not our actions are pleasing to God (John 7:24). Therefore, provided such actions are not abusive or exploitative, and do not violate another commitment (such as marriage or relationship with God), the morality or otherwise of sexual intimacy between two people of the same sex is, we believe, determined by their relationship with God, their love for one another, and a clear sense of personal responsibility towards their partner.[2]

Like Jeremy, I believe that any deed enacted without faith is sin (Romans 14:23). Therefore, however much I may want to be in agreement with Jeremy, because I believe sexual intimacy between members of the same sex is wrong, if I were to engage in homosexual behaviour holding such beliefs, I would be guilty of wilful sin. My fear of and love for God are too great to be jeopardised over such finite pleasure.

However, I do believe the issue to be greater than per-

---

1. www.courage.org.uk, Jeremy Marks, Newsletter, Spring 2001.
2. www.courage.org.uk, Jeremy Marks, "The Way Forward for Courage", December 2003.

sonal choice. *I must also state from the outset that I do not believe the Bible gives us permission, irrespective of personal attitude or motivation, to engage in homosexual behaviour.*

The Third Way

I have not married and produced children, and I have not returned to old ways of lesbian sexual relationships. So, am I destined to drift like some rootless nomad through the wilderness for the next 40 years? Will I be able to walk the "third way", no longer succumbing to the pressure of having to claim "healing" on the one hand or, on the other, arguing that homosexual behaviour is an acceptable expression of God's love?

The way I have walked and am walking is not easy and will be applauded by few. However, I do not believe that I am alone in this walk. I want to share with you the ways in which I have addressed this path so that you too can experience a "purposeful pilgrimage" and enter the Promised Land, rather than experiencing a "weary wandering" heading nowhere.

This book will not address the ongoing Christian and scientific debate on homosexuality. Current arguments can be followed through the written word and on the World Wide Web. It appears everyone has an opinion!

My aim is not to convince anyone of what they should believe, but simply to illustrate the path I have taken. My wish is that you become a fellow pilgrim on a lifelong journey.

He who would valiant be
'Gainst all disaster,
Let him in constancy
Follow the Master.
There's no discouragement
Shall make him once relent
His first avowed intent
To be a pilgrim.

          (John Bunyan [1628–1688])

Chapter One

What Is The Promised Land?

"Alex Davidson derives comfort in the midst of his homosexuality from his Christian hope. 'Isn't it one of the most wretched things about this condition,' he writes, 'that when you look ahead, the same impossible road seems to continue indefinitely? You're driven to rebellion when you think of there being no point to it and to despair when you think of there being no limit to it. That's why I find it a comfort, when I feel desperate, or rebellious, or both, to remind myself of God's promise that one day it will be finished...' "[3]

The Starting Point

God said to Abraham, "I will establish my covenant as an everlasting covenant between me and you and your descendants after you for the generations to come, to be your God and the God of your descendants after you. The whole land of Canaan, where you are now an alien, I will give as an everlasting possession to you and your descendants after you; and I will be their God" (Genesis 17:7f).

Centuries later, God clarified the promise of land to Moses. In Numbers 34:1–12a he cites in detail that the Hebrew homeland is to stretch from the Desert of Zin in the south to Riblah in the north. The eastern border was to begin

---

3. From *The Returns of Love*, InterVarsity Press, 1970, quoted in John Stott, *New Issues Facing Christians Today* (Marshall Pickering, London, 1999), page 416.

in Gilead, cross the River Jordan and stretch west until it reached the Mediterranean Sea. God concluded: "This will be your land, with its boundaries on every side" (Numbers 34:12b). God's allocation of land far exceeded that which was ever claimed by the twelve tribes in subsequent years. Even King David, great warrior that he was, never managed to claim the nation's full inheritance. Such is the magnitude of God's generosity.

The Promised Land certainly wasn't a place to sit back and take in the sights! True, it was a land of blessing, but it wasn't an empty land waiting for the Hebrews to inhabit at will: every conceivable adversary occupied the land. The Hebrews' land of blessing was a land of warfare. It didn't matter that they had trudged through the wilderness for the best part of 40 years. Without the warfare and subsequent victory, their inheritance would be left unclaimed. God had gifted them the land, yes, but it required effort and faithful obedience to conquer the enemies within and receive their legacy.

What's In It For Me?

The Hebrews' inheritance was very tangible. Thanks to God's clear direction, they knew the boundaries and the portion given to each tribe. The lowlands offered crops growing in abundance, while livestock grazed throughout the hill country. Indeed it was a land of plenty: the ground could be tilled, the water drunk, and the lakes and rivers fished.

But what does the term "Promised Land" suggest for us, Christians of the 21st century? If we don't know what the promise is, how will we know if and when it is ours to receive? If it isn't something as physical as land, then what are we to expect? And, just as importantly, what is expected of us when we get there?

Whether we admit it or not, some of the questions buzzing around in our head are: *What's in it for me? What is my reward? If I am to embark on a life of faithful commitment to God and his ways, what will I get in return? Will my journey and sacrifice be worth it?*

Without a clear understanding of the New Testament equivalent of the Promised Land, we will become discouraged amid life's difficulties and perhaps be tempted to turn back to Egypt.

Although any of the following is possible, our reward for a faithful walk away from homosexuality is not marriage and children, unambiguous heterosexuality or even a powerful life of ministry. Our reward is resting in God's perfect plan for our life.

God's Plan

God's plan is for each of us to be reconciled to him through the death and resurrection of his Son, Jesus. Not content with *mere* salvation, God's Holy Spirit wants to bring us into full redemption so that we may, as pastors of yesteryear would preach, "possess our possessions".

Salvation is all God's work. He did all the fighting for the Hebrews as they came out of Egypt; and Christ's propitiation secured our freedom from eternal death. Salvation is a free gift, but sanctification and growth in grace require effort if we are to claim all of our inheritance. It is not enough to be passive sheep waiting to be led to new pastures; we are to be trained and moulded into a fighting force ready to do the works God intends: "For it is by grace you have been saved, through faith – and this not from yourselves, it is the gift of God – not by works, so that no one can boast. For we are God's workmanship, created in Christ Jesus to do good works, which

God prepared in advance for us to do" (Ephesians 2:8–10). As the word "workmanship" sounds so mundane, I prefer to use another translation of the word. I find it more uplifting and encouraging to be known as God's "masterpiece", and this helps propel me towards further service in his name.

Is The Wilderness Necessary?

Much of the sanctification process is done in the wilderness. God's sovereign act freed the Hebrews from the bondage of Egypt. Their journey through the wilderness taught them to trust God for direction (by fire and cloud), sustenance (with manna and quail), and protection (from foreign armies). The Hebrews had to learn obedience, the meaning of holiness, the benefits of perseverance, and that the God they served is a righteous and jealous God who demands their complete worship.

The same is true for us. The sanctification process teaches and empowers us to say "No" to our old adamic nature and "Yes" to our re-creation in the image of Christ. God intends to bless us beyond all we can hope or imagine and create in us a heart filled with righteousness, peace, love and joy. He wants each believer to be conformed to the image of Jesus so that, one day, we will reign with him here on earth. God rests in the plan he has for us. Our call is to cease from fighting him and ourselves, and by faith enter into that rest.

Put simply, out of the learning to "be" in the wilderness, we are more able to "do" in the land. As we allow Jesus full rein in our lives, we become increasingly better equipped to fulfil God's purposes in our own life and serve him powerfully in the world.

Already Seated In The Heavenlies

Our position in Christ is assigned at conversion. We are seated in the heavenlies with him as co-heirs to an eternal inheritance. But it does not take us long to realise that our legal position, with Christ, and the position from which we operate are not necessarily the same! We read that God has given us all things through Christ: "Praise be to the God and Father of our Lord Jesus Christ, who has blessed us in the heavenly realms with every spiritual blessing in Christ" (Ephesians 1:3). Yet how often do we appear through our thoughts and actions not to fully possess these blessings? Daily bombardment from advertising on the television, in magazines, and on the side of the road, does little to keep the mind pure and fixed on Jesus. The proliferation of reality TV fosters voyeurism on a national scale; the viewer is encouraged vicariously to engage in "... sexual immorality, impurity and debauchery; idolatry and witchcraft; hatred, discord, jealousy, fits of rage, selfish ambition, dissensions, factions and envy; drunkenness, orgies, and the like" (Galatians 5:19–21).

The cult of celebrity can be intoxicating, and screaming headlines from the magazines at the supermarket checkout invite at least perusal, if not an impulse buy. One considers Internet pornography as a bastion of male sinfulness, but a recent magazine article tells a very different story. The editor introduces the item as follows: "34%. That's how many readers of *Today's Christian Woman*'s online newsletter admitted to intentionally accessing Internet porn in a recent poll. While many women wrote in to explain they'd accessed these sites to better understand what was luring their husbands time and again, it was the other e-mails – from Christian women who shared about their own Internet porn addiction – that caught our attention."[4]

---

4. Ramona Richards, "Dirty Little Secret", *Today's Christian Woman*, September/October 2003, Vol. 25, No. 5, page 58.

The article continues: "Women desiring to find companionship often prefer cybersex and online chat rooms to porn sites that offer only pictures and graphic stories, but they eventually start surfing both. All forms of pornography can stimulate the user, releasing chemicals in the brain that act on the body in much the same way as cocaine does. It's an exhilarating but unfortunately short-lived euphoria. The loneliness returns, leaving the woman wanting more contact and more stimulation, thus creating the cycle of addiction."

Armed with such depressing knowledge, and knowing that we are capable of the same, we could despair of ever maturing in the Lord. We could lose hope of closing the gap between our legal position in Christ and our daily walk with him. However, I find it encouraging that the apostle Paul, who penned the declaration in Ephesians 1:3, was also able to write: "So I find this law at work: When I want to do good, evil is right there with me. For in my inner being I delight in God's law; but I see another law at work in the members of my body, waging war against the law of my mind and making me a prisoner of the law of sin at work within my members. What a wretched man I am! Who will rescue me from this body of death?" (Romans 7:21–25a).

Our struggles may seem very 21st-century, but they are, in essence, no different from those of Paul. The solution, too, is exactly the same: "Thanks be to God – through Jesus Christ our Lord!" (Romans 7:25b). By bringing Christ into all circumstances and operating under the constraint of the Holy Spirit and with the power given through his indwelling, we are able to take power from the enemy's hands and claim land for God's kingdom. If we are willing, wilderness living will mould and shape our attitude. In time, our lives need not consist of pockets of holy passion weakened by intermittent apathy or rebellion, but will be trained and equipped and sold out to Jesus.

And what is the land we are to conquer? It is our heart, mind, soul and body. To enter God's rest requires conquering the sin that besets and entangles us, thus freeing each of us to minister according to God's purpose.

Purification prepares each believer for Christ's coming. Scripture states that without holiness we shall not see the Lord. In pursuing holy living and accomplishing righteous works we can live in the expectancy that when we see Jesus face to face we shall be like him. "Dear friends, now we are children of God, and what we will be has not yet been made known. But we know that when he appears, we shall be like him, for we shall see him as he is. Everyone who has this hope in him purifies himself, just as he is pure" (1 John 3:2f).

Today's Behaviour Dictates Tomorrow's Blessings

If we are born again by the Spirit of God, I believe that we have entered into an eternal relationship with our Father and should not fear judgment and eternal separation from him. However, I also believe that we will be judged according to what we have done with our salvation.

According to Revelation 19:8, we will be clothed in a garment made from our own righteous behaviour. I don't know about you, but my aim is not to struggle for eternity in some skimpy little number that barely covers my womanhood! I desire to bring my whole self into the will of God so that it is "not I who live, but Christ who lives in me" (Galatians 2:20b). In that way I can't help but act in a righteous manner in all things and to all people. Sadly, I fail with alarming frequency, but it is my desire to press on towards this goal.

This is why I do not condone homosexual behaviour. I do not believe that homosexual relationships, no matter if they are between "born again" Christians, no matter how monogamous, or self-giving, or steeped in prayer, can be regarded as righteous behaviour when the Bible's consistent moral teaching stipulates that sexual expression is to be confined within heterosexual marriage.

Unlike certain denominations, I also do not believe that the Bible differentiates between the behaviour of the clergy and that of the laity. It is my belief from 1 Peter 2:9 that we, clergy and laity alike, are "a priesthood of believers" equal before God, and should expect our moral lives to be judged with equal measure. We may not like the rules, but it is what we signed up for when we submitted our life to God. God has not moved the goalposts and neither should we.

Treasures In Heaven

Some rewards are immediate and some are gradually received as we mature in Christ. But the greatest rewards will be granted when we finally rule with Jesus on earth. If we fail to order our own lives now, or fall short of living a life pleasing to God and do not invest the "talents" we have been given, it seems unlikely that Jesus will give us much responsibility on the new earth. We must prove "faithful in the little" today so that we will be given much when we reign with Christ.

That is why in the midst of our struggles it is imperative that we retain an eternal perspective on our life and our call.

If your hope is to sit around drinking coffee and eating calorie-free chocolate for eternity, I hate to disappoint, but Jesus has work for us to do as co-heirs!

Jesus Hands Out His Reward

Jesus will reward those who have remained faithful to the call they were assigned while on earth. He is not overly concerned with our achievements and success stories, but whether we loved and trusted him enough to let Christ live unhindered in and through us.

In society's eyes we may have little to offer and in Christian circles we may be excluded from various aspects of service. Exclusion may be on the grounds of gender, as it is within certain denominations and groups, or it may be because of admitted difficulties in the area of sexuality.

Allow me to offer an illustration. Between seminars at a conference some years back, a rather distraught woman in her mid-20s approached me. In the previous class, I had been talking about the benefit of sharing with trusted church members one's lesbian struggles in order to receive support, understanding and encouragement. She explained that she was a relatively new Christian, a single mother of a two-year-old girl, and had broken off the relationship with her female partner soon after conversion because she felt it didn't tie in with her newfound faith. Because she was shy, the woman (we'll call her Wendy) decided to volunteer for crèche duty. In that way she was with her daughter and could get to know the other helpers in a safe environment. It was a ministry Wendy thoroughly enjoyed.

After a number of months, as various issues surfaced, Wendy decided she needed support and encouragement. The pastor seemed friendly and committed to his congregation, so Wendy made an appointment to see him. Although a little taken aback by her homosexual revelations, the pastor was affirming and said he would pray for her. However, Wendy was crushed when he also forbade her from serving in the crèche and in any other ministry to children. His reason? He wanted to protect the children in case she "led them astray" with her deviant thoughts and desires! Wendy was even forbidden to be in the crèche with her own daughter!

Sadly, this ignorant response, that those who experience homosexual feelings are potential child-abusers, is quite common. Is it any wonder homosexual men and women are reluctant to speak?

Fortunately, when we come to Jesus we receive justice. Irrespective of how much or how little you have achieved either in the world or in the church, if you have been faithful and diligent, and have persevered with your Christian discipleship during your earthly life, Jesus will reward you eternally with a position of authority and give you responsibilities and power to continue your service.

Not An Easy Walk

"Therefore, since we are surrounded by such a great cloud of witnesses, let us throw off everything that hinders and the sin that so easily entangles, and let us run with perseverance the race marked out for us" (Hebrews 12:1).

What is your race? I liken mine to the steeplechase, a track event requiring the runner to jump 35 three-foot barriers including a water jump before crossing the finishing line. To the athlete each barrier seems designed to rob you of energy and trip you up! The 3,000-metre race tests the runner's determination, stamina and, ultimately, finishing sprint. Jostling, elbowing and pushing appear de rigueur, although team mates from the same country offer some protection from rivals during the race's duration.

I'd like to think that the race God has marked out for me is not only an individual event, but requires an element of teamwork so that we can all complete the course.

Addressing one's homosexuality is no easy matter. The journey requires leaving Egypt, travelling through the wilderness, and having the courage to enter the Promised

Land. It is a journey beset with hurdles, barriers and water jumps. However, it is not a journey that need be travelled alone. "See to it, [sisters], that none of you has a sinful, unbelieving heart that turns away from the living God. But encourage one another daily, as long as it is called Today, so that none of you may be hardened by sin's deceitfulness. We have come to share in Christ if we *hold firmly till the end* the confidence we had at first" (Hebrews 3:12–14, emphasis mine).

It is my desire that each of us completes this endurance race and comes to know God's rest. But, before we can enter the Promised Land and conquer the strongholds ahead, it is necessary to adopt the right attitude. We need to cultivate the mind of a pilgrim.

Chapter Two

Purposeful Pilgrimage

"Without the Way, there is no going; without the Truth,
there is no knowing; without the Life, there is no living."
Thomas à Kempis, *The Imitation of Christ*

Pilgrimage For All?

The term "pilgrimage" conjures up a number of pictures in people's minds. We think of the tens of thousands of Muslims who flock to Mecca each year; or the thousands of Hindus scattered along the banks of the Ganges; or the many Catholics who travel to Lourdes. Rarely do we consider ourselves as participants.

Yet, even in our turbulent lives, we often seek refuge in the presence of God. This may be through a church service, a moment of quiet in a park, or in the lonely hours of the night. Whatever outward expression a person makes, a pilgrimage is all about someone moving towards God. Why do we do it? The book of Ecclesiastes states: "He has also set eternity in the hearts of men" (Ecclesiastes 3:11). There is an inner compulsion instigated by God who calls us on the journey. There is a cost. In order to be a pilgrim, we must leave what is known and comfortable and follow the ways that bring us to ever-increasing and deepening faith.

The philosopher Socrates stated that an unexamined life is not worth living. Choosing to address our homosexuality with the heart of a pilgrim gives us the opportunity to make two journeys: the first an inner journey pursuing a mature relationship with God, thus equipping us for the second, outer journey, that of service in his name.

Package-tour Pilgrim

Clutching my camera in one hand and Walkman in the other, I boarded the coach in Christchurch, New Zealand. Before me lay a two-week journey around the South Island, taking in the cities of Dunedin and Invercargill, the awe-inspiring beauty of Milford Sound, and culminating with the exhilaration of skiing down Mount Cook. I intended to participate fully in the experience.

After a few days, I had fallen into a soporific state. One sight blended into another, each meal became indistinguishable from the last, and conversation with my fellow travellers had long since ceased to have meaning. The only responsibility I had was to get up on time, leave my suitcase with the driver, eat breakfast, and board the coach. Unwittingly, I had adopted the air of one institutionalised. Sadly, I remember little of my holiday in New Zealand.

Backpacking is altogether a different affair from a package tour. Organising the route, visas and necessary inoculations, the tickets and itinerary, requires one's full attention. Depending on where you go, there can be dangers involved in your travel: the risks of catching malaria or experiencing dysentery tend to focus the mind! And unexpectedly encountering the redback spider under your toilet lid is certainly stimulating.

But backpacking is not always about action; there can be a lot of waiting around. To be informed that there is a bus to your next destination is encouraging, but to be told it won't arrive for another three days requires patience and a certain amount of creative thought.

A backpacker is opportunistic. Flexibility is all-important and one needs to be ready for the occasional setback: a hurricane, a train strike, not knowing the language properly, getting used to different customs and being willing to experiment with different foods. For the most part, it means letting go of preconceived ideas and going with the flow.

As a Christian, it is easy to adopt a "package-tour" mentality and let the pastor and elders take the responsibility for running your life. It is easy to abdicate responsibility for your journey and just go along for the ride. Conversely, backpacking and, therefore, pilgrimage, requires knowing your ultimate destination without being too sure how you are going to get there. It's about travelling light and being able to respond to any situation one encounters. To engage successfully in a pilgrimage one needs a pioneer spirit, one that is willing to learn and explore.

In a package tour, you pay your money and let everyone else do the work. When one embarks on a pilgrimage the onus is on *you* to prepare, organise and actively participate in its success.

Even Package Tours Can Go Wrong

What is wrong with having a "package-tour" mentality? We may want to opt for an easy Christian life: attend church on a Sunday, attend mid-week Bible study, sign up for one of the rotas, and pay our tithe. On the surface everything seems fine. As far as you are concerned, you have signed up for the package deal and the next stop is heaven. But even package tours can go wrong.

Imagine that you want to holiday in Spain. You have bought your ticket, turn up at London Gatwick, wait in the departure lounge, and finally board the plane. It's not up to you how the plane is flown – the only choice you have to make is in your selection of food and whether or not to read the in-flight magazine. As far as you are concerned, the only time you next need to think is once you have cleared customs and leave the airport terminal.

But what happens if you are hijacked?

All preconceived expectations are in turmoil. Suddenly thrown back on your own resources, how will you deal with the situation? You may not have freedom of movement or be physically able to change the situation, but your mental ability to cope with the radical change of plan is put to the test. Faced with the unexpected, panic can occur. How often our nice, simple Christian walk can be hijacked!

This applies to the issue of lesbianism. The healing that we have diligently prayed for appears not to be taking place. Worse than that, we find ourselves drawn into an emotional involvement with another woman, or, to our horror, we find that the relationship is becoming physical. This was not our intention; this was not on the itinerary. Where has our long-term plan of slotting into conventional Christian life gone?

The Bible passages we once looked to for comfort now appear cold and lifeless. The praise and worship in church leave us feeling alienated from those to whom we once felt bonded. Sermons don't even begin to address the issues we are facing. Other people's simple trust and faith grate on our nerves. *Where has it all gone wrong? How have I ended up here? When will this struggle end?*

What is exposed when God shines his light on your life? Does he see a woman hungering after intimacy with him, or does he see a dispirited woman settling for a comfortable, if quiet, life of acceptance within "church"?

When we face struggle, temptation and doubt, we will see not only the poverty of our spiritual walk, but also the opportunity to take up our backpack and, like Christian in *The Pilgrim's Progress*, head out toward the Celestial City.

Old Testament Characters

One doesn't have to read too much of the Bible to recognise the proliferation of pilgrims in the Old Testament. Book after book is littered with people who hear the call of God on their lives and respond to that call. A cursory glance at the Bible offers us the likes of Abraham, Moses, Joshua and the prophets, who all left stable environments and, trusting only in God's Word, literally travelled hundreds of miles in order to fulfil his call on their life. Their personal pilgrimage of faith resulted in an external pilgrimage.

Although each of them worked out their call in different ways and with different results, they all had a common goal. Their attitude and heartfelt desire was to hear, seek out and walk towards God. The Old Testament points towards the coming of the Messiah and the salvation of God's people. None of the characters ever experienced that moment, yet, despite some deviations off the path, none were ultimately deterred from fulfilling God's call on their lives.

All these people were still living by faith when they died. They did not receive the things promised; they only saw them and welcomed them from a distance. And they admitted that they were aliens and strangers on earth. People who say such things show that they are looking for a country of their own. If they had been thinking of the country they had left, they would have had opportunity to return. Instead, they were longing for a better country – a heavenly one. Therefore God is not ashamed to be called their God, for he has prepared a city for them. (Hebrews 11:13)

God The Pilgrim

Since we live after Jesus' walk on the earth, is our call any different? Yes, and no. The same call given to the pilgrim is given to us: we are to find God. It is different in as much as we have already received God through Christ, and in us dwells the Holy Spirit. He guides and walks with each of us towards the Father, so, in that respect, we could say that God too has become a pilgrim.

Do you find the challenge to pilgrimage too difficult or frightening? Be encouraged: pilgrimage is not our idea. We did not set out to find Jesus, but Jesus came to seek us, the sinners. He still comes to seek us out, to empower us and to walk with us towards the Father. We have a very important decision to make. Either we respond to this call and walk with him, or we ignore the call and walk away from him.

However difficult the path, remember that we are not left alone to stumble through life. Let us be mindful of the scripture: "... the glorious riches of this mystery, which is Christ in you, the hope of glory" (Colossians 1:27).

Because the letter to the Hebrews says that Jesus is God Incarnate, we know that he can identify with us. He knows our humanness and weaknesses. Your path may be hard, but it is manageable. Dietrich Bonhoeffer said, "The most important thing is keeping God's pace, trying neither to precede him nor to stay behind." Be encouraged: Jesus is Immanuel – "God with us".

An Active Life

I believe the call to pilgrimage in the New Testament can be found in Paul's statement: "Continue to work out your salvation with fear and trembling" (Philippians 2:12b).

This has nothing to do with being saved or unsaved, but with the consequence of becoming a Christian. Salvation is a gift, but what do we do with it? Jesus says that we are called by name and for a purpose. Our responsibility is to find out what that purpose is. We are given two important commands. The first is to love the Lord with our heart and mind, and the second is to love others as oneself. We can only love others biblically if we fulfil the first part, loving God correctly.

The more we know God and his character, the more we will love him. As we continually open up to the love that is on offer, we will have a greater sense of security. Only out of that security can we acquire a pilgrim heart that isn't afraid to walk to the edge and explore the nuances of our faith and purpose.

A sense of insecurity will only foster a desire to seek refuge. For many, that will mean seeking refuge in relationships that encourage our lesbian inclination, or, out of fear of sinning, we may spurn friendship and lose ourselves in good works or ministry. But security does not come through friendships, no matter how pure they may be; neither is it found on the mission field. True security is only finally understood when a person has slid down life's ladder and found Jesus there, holding it steady.

Travelling Light, Travelling Appropriately

In my late teens, I worked at an outdoor pursuit centre in Wales. This centre offered a week-long introduction to activities such as potholing, rock climbing and sea canoeing. An overnight camping trip was also planned where the children had to carry their rucksacks with all their personal belongings. We were kind to them, so the food, tents and sleeping bags went ahead in the Land Rovers. The children were encouraged to pack what they deemed necessary for the trip, bearing in mind that the six-mile walk was over the challenging Brecon Beacons.

On one occasion, there was a group of girls who seemed to have full rucksacks and continually lagged behind the other children. At camp, they were late for the meeting around the fire, so I went to their tent to find the reason for the delay.

To my astonishment, they were putting on make-up and doing their hair. Around them in the overcrowded tent were several selections of tops and jeans, and two unused hairdryers. The girls were dismayed by the lack of mains sockets in that particular area of Wales! Of course, not only were their accessories useless for the night, they had to turn round and carry them back a further six miles the next day.

Perhaps we are more mature than these girls, but what kind of unnecessary baggage are we carrying with us on our pilgrimage? Are you labouring under the burden of failure? Had you hoped, expected, even prayed to feel different from how you do today? Has the hoped-for change in orientation not materialised? Do you feel second-rate? Do you feel even more unacceptable today than you did when you first addressed your homosexuality? Are you afraid to tell your friends, pastor and congregation that, despite your years of trying, you are no nearer gliding up the aisle attired in shimmering white than you were ten years ago?

It is time to get rid of the baggage.

Helpful Hints

"Since, then, you have been raised with Christ, set your hearts on things above, where Christ is seated at the right hand of

God. Set your minds on things above, not on earthly things" (Colossians 3:1f).

The New Testament is full of attitudes that we are either to take off or put on. All of these will help us in our walk towards God. The list is almost endless. You may wish to consider the following scriptures:

> For this very reason, make every effort to add to your faith goodness; and to goodness, knowledge; and to knowledge, self-control; and to self-control, perseverance; and to perseverance, godliness; and to godliness, brotherly kindness; and to brotherly kindness, love. For if you possess these qualities in increasing measure, they will keep you from being ineffective and unproductive in your knowledge of our Lord Jesus Christ. (2 Peter 1:5–8)

> Put to death, therefore, whatever belongs to your earthly nature: sexual immorality, impurity, lust, evil desires and greed, which is idolatry. Because of these, the wrath of God is coming. You used to walk in these ways, in the life you once lived. But now you must rid yourselves of all such things as these: anger, rage, malice, slander and filthy language from your lips. Do not lie to each other, since you have taken off your old self with its practices and have put on the new self, which is being renewed in knowledge in the image of its Creator. (Colossians 3:5–10)

> So I say, live by the Spirit, and you will not gratify the desires of the sinful nature. For the sinful nature desires what is contrary to the Spirit, and the Spirit what is contrary to the sinful nature. They are in conflict with each other, so that you do not do what you want. But if you are led by the Spirit, you are not under the law.
>
> The acts of the sinful nature are obvious: sexual immorality, impurity and debauchery; idolatry and witchcraft; hatred,

discord, jealousy, fits of rage, selfish ambition, dissensions, factions and envy; drunkenness, orgies, and the like. I warn you, as I did before, that those who live like this will not inherit the kingdom of God.

But the fruit of the Spirit is love, joy, peace, patience, kindness, goodness, faithfulness, gentleness and self-control. Against such things there is no law. Those who belong to Christ Jesus have crucified the sinful nature with its passions and desires. Since we live by the Spirit, let us keep in step with the Spirit. (Galatians 5:16–25)

Things To Ask Yourself

What is my attitude towards my Christian life? Did I begin with an open ticket around the world, excited by the prospect of adventure, and, somewhere along the line, trade it in for a two-week all-inclusive package holiday?

Am I content to toe the party line, claiming an "ex-gay" stance? Or do I want to break free from the self-imposed shackles, admit my ongoing struggles, and explore the freedom of being *real* in Christ?

Where is my security? Have I entered God's rest and do I know that I am being faithful to his call on my life?

Am I prepared to accept some things and reject others? Do I have the courage to stand against the tide of public opinion?

Is there anything in my life that draws me back to Egypt?

We may have left Egypt many years ago, but that doesn't mean that Egypt has left us. Are there some nuggets of your past life that you still carry around in your pocket and use almost like a comforter when faced with certain stressors?

Chapter Three

The Treasures
Of Egypt

"As long as you run from where you are and distract yourself, you cannot fully let yourself be healed."[5]

Tipper was one of a kind. A dog from an animal shelter, he had never fully grasped the concept of house training, nor had he cast aside his scavenging ways, despite being well fed and cared for. He loved playing on the beach and regularly brought back his trophies for me to admire. On one occasion, he returned parading a large, decaying and extremely smelly fish clasped firmly between his jaws. The temptation to abandon him was great! Nothing would persuade Tipper to part with his treasure, and walking along the promenade back to the car was an embarrassment. People stared, covered their mouths and noses, and veered violently out of the way as Tipper trotted proudly at my side. Between waves of nausea, I was frantically trying to figure out how to avoid taking the fish home.

Then I saw the ice cream van. Tipper loved ice cream. Would he give up the fish for a cornet? It was my only chance. We must have seemed an odd couple: he with a decaying carcass hanging out of his mouth and me with cheap ice cream rapidly melting down my hand, begging him to "drop". What a dilemma for Tipper! He knew that he had to surrender one in favour of the other and yet he liked both. Fortunately for

5. Henri J M Nouwen, *The Inner Voice of Love* (Image Books, New York, 1998), page 31.

all concerned, the ice cream won. However, I have to say, the smell of fish lingered for a long time after!

The "dog" incident reminded me of a gloriously simple dog illustration that Anne, a pastor's wife and fellow teacher, once offered, representing the difference between living life without Christ and a life with him. "Consider a dog in a backyard," she said. "She is happy gnawing on her old bone, content with what she has. But what dog would not leave that bone if the master appeared at the door offering her a piece of rump steak?"

Tired Of The Atkins Diet?

Do you feel as though you are on a carbohydrate-free diet? At some point did you leave the bone of lesbian behaviour and accept the offer of new life from the Master? You left a life of reasonable contentment for something you believed was best: obedience to Christ. And how are you feeling now? In your estimation, has the "best" measured up to the promise? Or is your heart turning back to Egypt?

The Hebrews complained: "If only we had meat to eat! We remember the fish we ate in Egypt at no cost – also the cucumbers, melons, leeks, onions and garlic. But now we have lost our appetite; we never see anything but this manna!" (Numbers 11:4–6). Their cries of discontent directly contrast with the single vision of Moses: "He regarded disgrace for the sake of Christ as of greater value than *the treasures of Egypt*, because he was looking ahead to his reward" (Hebrews 11:26, emphasis mine).

What are the "treasures of Egypt?" Like many of us, the Hebrews were guilty of selective memory. Conveniently, they had forgotten their position of slavery in Egypt and that God's actions were in response to their cries for help (Exodus

3:7–10)! They were chosen by God and freed from slavery, yet promises of their own country paled into insignificance; all the people could think about was the variety of food they had left behind.

In A Pickle Over Pickle

I have a certain amount of sympathy with the Hebrews' plight. Food memories are very evocative and often produce feelings of security and better times. They can awaken individual determination like nothing else. After living in California for a few months, all I craved was a cheese and Branston pickle sandwich. As much as I tried to make do with their numerous American pickles, none could satisfy the increasing "need" for real Branston pickle. Over the weeks I became increasingly cranky and obsessive. Finally, in desperation, I took an hour's drive into San Francisco, paid the toll booth to cross the Golden Gate Bridge, pumped an excessive number of coins into a parking meter, and then shelled out an extortionate amount of money at an English food outlet: all this effort for a *small* jar of pickle. My precious "treasure" had cost me half a day and nearly £25. And was the effort worth it? Unfortunately, I have no recollection of that first "branstonised" cheese sandwich!

We may scoff at the Hebrews' inability to grasp the bigger picture and their focus on areas of immediate gratification, but aren't we guilty of something similar? What are your "treasures of Egypt"? What makes you glance back at your past with a certain longing? Would it be in the area of relationships? Do you miss the intimacy of that one "special other"?

Perhaps the "treasure of Egypt" you yearn for is being able to indulge your emotions without feeling obliged to keep them in check. Pandering to emotional fantasy can take the edge off the reality you are experiencing. Bringing each thought captive (2 Corinthians 10:5) is exhausting, and sometimes you long for a day off!

Your "treasure" could be the freedom of movement you enjoyed, literally as well as emotionally. Perhaps you had the ready company of like-minded people who were single and available to enjoy activities at a moment's notice. Memories of those times can be in stark contrast to the poverty of same-age/same-interest/same-freedom relationships you now possess.

The sexual aspect of any relationship could also be the "treasure of Egypt" you miss most. All I can say is that the longer one is celibate, the less demanding and acute the sexual desire becomes.

Swimming Uphill

Deciding to swim against the tide of public opinion produces opposition from all sides. My doctor wishes that he could wave a wand so I could live life fully as a lesbian and as a Christian. Most Christians want me to be able to declare that I am a new creation in Christ with heterosexuality at the top of the new creative order! Then there are those Christians who believe that homosexual behaviour is another expression of God's love and just want me to find a partner and "be happy".

What is the answer? What enables me not to value the "treasures of Egypt" above the treasures of heaven?

"Do not store up for yourselves treasures on earth, where moth and rust destroy, and where thieves break in and steal. But store up for yourselves treasures in heaven, where moth and rust do not destroy, and where thieves do not break in and steal. For where your treasure is, there your heart will be also" (Matthew 6:19–21). Jesus is clearly talking about money in this passage. However, the concept is transferable. Consider the Hebrews back in Egypt. When Moses asked Pharaoh to let everyone go in order to worship the Lord, Pharaoh demonstrated an astute understanding regarding the pull of relationships on the heart. He offered a compromise: "Pharaoh said, 'The Lord be with you – if I let you go, along with your women and children! Clearly you are bent on evil. No! Let only the men go; and worship the Lord, since that's what you have been asking for.' Then Moses and Aaron were driven out of Pharaoh's presence" (Exodus 10:10f).

Pharaoh understood human nature. He knew that the men would not abandon their wives and children in Egypt while they themselves escaped from the clutches of slavery. He reckoned that the pull of human relationships would keep them firmly in his grasp, no matter how great their desire to worship God.

Is it the pull of relationship, past, present or future, that is causing you to waver in your commitment? Personally, as a single 40-something, I find it hard to foster good relationships as most women in my church are married and/or with children. Understandably their priorities are not mine, and I am, at best, fourth or fifth down the pecking order when it comes to time and emotional investment. Spontaneous acts of pleasure, such as a trip to the movies, are virtually non-existent. In my lonely moments, it requires effort not to recall my past through rose-tinted spectacles. Satan would have us believe that those halcyon days were just bursting with activity, love, fun and excitement! However good or not those days in "Egypt" actually were, we must refrain from indulgence. For a path of compromise may just be offered!

Let us reconsider the text from Hebrews: "He [Moses] regarded disgrace for the sake of Christ as of greater value than *the treasures of Egypt*, because he was looking ahead to his reward" (Hebrews 11:26, emphasis mine). Moses enjoyed a privileged life as the adopted son of Pharaoh. He had first-hand knowledge of wealth and power, and experienced all the advantages identified with a royal upbringing. But from this vantage point, Moses understood the transitory nature of such freedom. He knew that earthly treasure, be it relational or material, will get broken or stolen or just rust away over the years. At one time the Egyptian empire was formidable and feared by all, yet today it is merely a topic studied by children in school. Looking beyond the immediate, Moses decided not to indulge in the riches on offer, preferring the constraint of obedience to God.

Like Moses, we need to live in the here-and-now in the light of the future. The "treasures of Egypt" are finite at best, unreliable, and can prove to be very painful. Indulging in these treasures puts at risk God's plans to bless us both on earth and for eternity. Settling for the temporal prevents us from experiencing the full blessings found in God.

What Planet Are You On?

The life we are living is not all there is. We are called to be aliens and strangers on this earth. It is time to accept that we are not living according to the rules of this world or of certain factions within the Christian church.

Christian society demands that we conform to its way of thinking as much as secular society. While I am not promoting unbridled rebellion in the pews, I am encouraging you to walk in accordance with biblical standards and the witness of the Holy Spirit. Test everything. Is the teaching that you are hearing founded in Scripture or does it offer rather appealing, liberal views? Perhaps the converse is true. Consider the preaching you hear and the church ethos you live under. Are they biblically true or merely offering conservative Christian niceties? Are you only encouraged to live a safe, obedient life headed up by marriage, children and a "happy-ever-after" feel?

God doesn't live in a nice tidy box, and neither should we. Married or single, with or without children, let us embrace the pioneer spirit! Let us live as aliens, unsettle the status quo, and find out who this God is who demands all that we have and all that we are.

When I stand before God's throne of judgment, I will not be asked about the attitude and behaviour of others. I will be asked how I worked out the gift of salvation given to me. Did I invest well or did I squander the gift? Did I return to Egypt frustrated with the outcome of my wilderness wanderings? Was I content to be a settler in a strange land or did I press on as a pilgrim on the road to holiness? Did I claim at least some of the Promised Land during my life on earth?

Pilgrimage Through The Wilderness

Escape from Egypt came about in a comparatively short space of time. But it took nearly 40 years to get Egypt out of the Hebrews. Indeed, none of the adult escapees, except Joshua and Caleb, succeeded in embracing God's way; they all died in the desert, never having fulfilled God's purpose for them. It was up to the second and subsequent generations to submit to God and successfully distinguish his voice from all others. They had their moments of commitment, but in truth, the children and grandchildren were no more obedient to God than their forefathers.

If I am to live fully in the Promised Land, it is imperative that I try to remove all traces of Egypt from within. The wilderness strips us of all the paraphernalia that clogs our life emotionally, physically and spiritually. We are exposed before our Maker and before ourselves. That which we once relied upon is removed. I long to hear the voice of Jesus say, "Well done, my good and faithful servant." It is that desire which propels me forward in my Christianity. But in order not to look back over my shoulder at Egypt or be content with the mediocrity of living east of the Jordan, I need to ensure that my heart is strong enough for the journey, and that I am ready to hear his voice.

"Therefore, behold, I will allure her [Israel] and bring her into the wilderness, and I will speak tenderly and to her heart" (Hosea 2:14, Amplified Bible).

Chapter Four

Coronary Care

"As God entrusts us with more responsibility, the hardships may increase as well. Feelings of abandonment intensify, any sense of the presence of God fades, and temptations and doubts multiply. Henri Nouwen coined a daring phrase, 'the ministry of absence', and advised that we do a disservice if we witness only to God's presence and do not prepare others to experience the times when God seems absent."[6]

Raised in the Catholic faith, I vividly remember statues standing at various points throughout the church building. One such figure was called the "Sacred Heart". A life-size image of Jesus stood on a plinth, towering over the kneeling Christian. Christ looked down, his white garment ripped open to reveal a heart encompassed by thorns. The message was clear. Jesus' heart, although injured by our sin, nevertheless remains exposed, accessible and full of love. Indeed, the gospels tell of Christ's compassion and subsequent suffering for the lost, and the Scriptures clearly state that, despite the pain endured, Jesus remained open to his Father and to others. Our call is no different.

Pilgrimage requires a firm resolve if we are to complete the journey. The wilderness is designed to challenge our core beliefs, attitudes and behaviours, bringing each into line with God's design. Our belief, attitude and behaviour should image that of Jesus, as laid out in Philippians 4:1–8.

---

6. Philip Yancey, *Reaching for the Invisible God* (Zondervan, Grand Rapids, 2000), page 241.

In the wilderness, pilgrims are offered a chance to sink their roots of faith deep into Jesus or be tossed around the arid landscape like a piece of tumbleweed. The wilderness is a place of hardship but, more importantly, *it is a place of opportunity*. It presents the chance to get our heart right before God, thus preparing us for unwavering service.

> Like Israel, we may enter the gateway to the Promised Land with all the treasures of Egypt, but we will have to learn to depend on the Lord for even a drink of water. It is in the wilderness that He is made our Lord and we become His priests. It is there that we become intimate with Him and learn His ways. There the facades of our old nature are stripped away, and we come to know how desperately we need the transformation He is working in us.[7]

Wilderness walking will expose our hearts, not for destructive purposes, even though the process may involve pain, but in order to create an undivided heart.

The Hebrews assigned the important functions of life to different physical organs. The heart was considered the core of a person's intellectual and spiritual function. The prophet Jeremiah pulls no punches in describing its state: "The heart is deceitful above all things and beyond cure" (Jeremiah 17:9). Yet there is so much more to the heart than its ability to deceive. It is easily hurt (Psalm 109:22), yet can be strengthened (Deuteronomy 30:4–6). God speaks to the heart (Nehemiah 7:5), and he changes it (Ezekiel 11:19). He searches the heart (Proverbs 17:10) and fills it with himself (Psalm 4:7). God calls us to repent from the heart (Psalm 18:30–32) and to avoid wrong attitudes (Proverbs 23:17). Our heart is to seek out the purposes of God (Acts 1:24).

---

7. Rick Joyner, *The Journey Begins* (Whitaker House, New Kensington, PA, 1997), page 38.

The Guarded And Unguarded Heart

Scripture instructs us to guard our heart because it is the wellspring of life (Proverbs 4:23). This means that we are not to entertain situations or people who may entice us away from the nurture of an undivided heart towards the Lord Jesus. However, we also have to live with an unguarded heart, meaning that we relinquish our vain attempts at self-protection in favour of Christ's offer of protection. We actively live according to the Bible's promise: God is the tower we run to (Psalm 61:3), he is our refuge (Psalm 9:9), and he is the shield we can hide behind (Proverbs 2:7f).

How unguarded is your heart towards Jesus? Are you more secure when "doing" for Jesus rather than "being" with him? Is it important to you to present a capable, unflappable image to Jesus rather than offering him the more vulnerable aspects of your personality? In your quiet times, do you live in the safety of your head rather than let the uncertainty of your emotions have a voice? Are you better at interceding for others than making your requests known to God?

The unguarded place we need to stand in is not in our minds, but in our hearts. In his book *Waiting on God*, Andrew Murray wrote this: "It is with the heart man believes and comes into touch with God, it is in the heart God has given his spirit to be there to us as the presence and power of God working in us. In all our religion, the heart must trust, love, and worship and obey. My mind is utterly impotent in creating and maintaining a spiritual life within me. The heart must wait on God to work in me."[8]

In an age of reasoned Christianity, it is easy to overlook the importance of the heart. Many women, seeking to pursue

---

8. Andrew Murray, *Waiting on God* (Moody Press, 1990), page 51.

pilgrimage, see the heart as weak and an encumbrance rather than as helpful in knowing God at a more intimate level.

Even if we trust God with our heart and emotions, we may be wary of our own or other people's emotional response. This can be very understandable, depending on our own life histories. In the past, we may have operated with few emotional boundaries and experienced a number of exhilarating yet ultimately painful emotional rollercoaster rides. In an effort not to wander back down a trail of homosexual responses, we may be dogged by our own doubt. Endless internal questions may plague us: *Am I entering into sin if I respond emotionally here? Am I walking down my old paths of living and responding or is this a healthy response to what is happening? Am I caring too much?*

Dealing with matters of the heart can be exhausting, and at times it may be tempting to close off and ignore the pounding in our chest. *Live in the head,* we conclude, *and get on with life.* However tempting it is to be dismissive, God considers our heart very important and continues to give it his full attention.

Heads, No One Wins

I was most adept at living within the confines of my head. Although I had experienced physically excruciating heart pain at my conversion, as I sensed God's hand on my chest spiritually changing a heart of stone into a heart of flesh (Ezekiel 36:26), I still lived well and truly within the confines of my mind. There was more than a mere 18-inch gap between my head and heart to contend with – there was a whole way of living to address. My faith, belief and growth in the Lord were largely headbound. Service emanated more from the head, meaning that I acted a certain way because "it was the right thing to do" rather than operating from the heart as illustrated by Jesus: "When he saw the crowds, he had compassion on them, because they were harassed and helpless, like sheep without a shepherd" (Matthew 9:36).

Obviously, there were some chinks in my heart armour, and emotions would fight for daylight. This would result in "leaky eyes", an ever-increasing lump in the throat and near-paralysing stress headaches.

As a result of the publication of my book, *Out of Egypt*, ministry opportunities increased from early 1991. By 1994 I was beginning to feel the strain, and although God was continuing to bless the work, I felt with each speaking engagement that parts of me were being ripped away. A journal entry of that time reads, *I feel like an empty shell, I look OK on the outside but I am hollow, like a cheap Easter egg. The shape is right and the coloured foil sparkles but the chocolate is too thin to withstand any knock. The shell will shatter and cave in.*

Irregular Heart Rhythm

Perhaps you are extremely aware of your heart response. Life may be jogging along quite nicely, when all of a sudden your heart suffers from a spiritual irregular rhythm. Are there times when your stance on homosexual behaviour derails? You understand the case for sexual abstinence perfectly well, and behaviourally comply, but experience an internal rage against the prohibition. There is external submission but heart rebellion.

"Just believing in our minds does not accomplish anything unless that knowledge is transferred to our hearts. That transfer from head to heart is always reflected in how we live – especially by how we live when we are under pressure or in the midst of trials. The Lord said, 'They go astray in their heart,' not their mind."

"When we go astray, it is seldom in our minds but in our hearts. We can accurately believe all doctrine yet not live any of it. We can have the Bible memorized and yet be rebels. Many of us believe God in our minds but not in our hearts, 'For with the heart man believes, resulting in righteousness' (Romans 10:10)."[9]

Wilderness wandering provides the chance to expose those pockets of rebellion that have taken root in the heart. Our subsequent repentance and invitation for Jesus to extend his reign in our lives brings us that much closer to the Promised Land. Be encouraged! I don't know how many times you don't do the things you intend to, and say and do things which you later regret; it is easy to live in a state of self-condemnation. Therefore, it is good to remind ourselves of God's compassion: "...and serve him with wholehearted devotion and with a willing mind, for the Lord searches every heart and understands every motive behind the thoughts" (1 Chronicles 28:9). I am truly glad that he can decipher the good intention behind the bad action!

Remembering God's compassion may help us give more leeway to our heart reaction.

Point Of Access

Although Satan entered the mind of Judas, encouraging the betrayal of his Master, God's direct line of access to us is not through the mind, but through the heart. Consider the verse in Acts: "One of those listening was a woman named Lydia, a

9. Rick Joyner, *The Journey Begins* (Whitaker House, New Kensington, PA, 1997), page 109.

dealer in purple cloth from the city of Thyatira, who was a worshipper of God. The Lord opened her heart to respond to Paul's message" (Acts 16:14). The passage does not say, "Lydia thought this was a great idea and responded to Paul's message," but that God opened her heart, and her heart responded. She did not stop to think out the logic of Paul's teaching, but God opened up the space in her life for himself. What is God's simple message to us? It must be that he wants a relationship built upon him who is love. Intelligence is great and certainly has a place, but to have an open heart to him is of greater worth.

Although Lydia placed herself in order to hear Paul, the passage implies a certain passivity on her part. The same is true for us. God himself opens our heart and, according to Romans 5:5, "God has poured out his love into our hearts by the Holy Spirit, whom he has given us." Even if our mind is slow in understanding God's ways, we can be confident that there is opportunity to have our hearts filled *and* overflowing with his love.

Not only does God speak to our hearts, he actually takes up residence in them (2 Corinthians 1:21f). When our minds begin to doubt and question aspects of our pilgrimage, we can rest assured that our heart is sealed and God's Holy Spirit resides as a deposit of what is to come. Whether I am aware of it or not, my heart has become totally accessible to God. An acceptance of that truth can produce a sense of fear as well as comfort.

With reference to our lesbianism, *full-heart acceptance* that God forbids sexual expression empowers us to move forwards in our Christian journey irrespective of the temptations we may face. When something is only understood as a "good idea" or seen as "the right thing to do", then we are open to doubt and ultimately may be swayed from our path.

Is My Heart Oblivious To God?

We may be unaware of the daily presence of God in our lives for a variety of reasons. Merely doffing our cap in acknowledgment of God rather than inviting him in to be central to our lives produces an unhealthy independence. Before long, we may become insensitive to his voice. But all is not lost. "Rend your heart and not your garments. Return to the Lord your God, for he is gracious and compassionate, slow to anger and abounding in love, and he relents from sending calamity" (Joel 2:13). "Because your heart was responsive and you humbled yourself... I have heard you... " (2 Kings 22:19). When we hear God with a humble heart, nothing can break that line of communication.

Along with humility, we need wisdom. Are you wise in your decision-making? Are you wise in the company you are keeping, the websites you are visiting, or the articles you are reading? God placed wisdom in Solomon's heart (1 Kings 10:24), and the apostle Paul prayed that the Ephesians would have the Spirit of wisdom (Ephesians 1:17). Therefore, we can pray with confidence for wisdom to know God better and act in keeping with that knowledge.

If we have been addressing our homosexuality for any length of time, we will be well versed in the passage telling us to "take every thought captive" (2 Corinthians 10:5). However, training our minds is exhausting and our willpower can fail. Unless our hearts are convinced of God's call to sexual restraint concerning homosexuality, there is a great possibility that we will slide into sin.

Therefore, we would do well to follow the writer of Hebrews, who says: "See to it, [sisters], that none of you has a sinful, unbelieving heart that turns away from the living God. But encourage one another daily, as long as it is called Today, so that none of you may be hardened by sin's deceitfulness" (Hebrews 3:12). We all have an enemy who will, in one breath, encourage us in his ways, and then, in the next breath, condemn us for entertaining such thoughts. Let us not grow weary of encouraging one another in Christ.

Is My Heart The Enemy?

While not denying the scriptures that warn of the fickleness of the heart, it would be wrong to view our heart as the enemy. The Bible has much more to say about its frailty and potential to bless than about its tendency to lead us astray.

Proverbs speaks of the heart with great insight: "An anxious heart weighs a man down, but a kind word cheers him up" (Proverbs 12:25). "Hope deferred makes the heart sick, but a longing fulfilled is a tree of life" (Proverbs 13:12). "Even in laughter, the heart may ache, and joy may end in grief" (Proverbs 14:13). "Each heart knows its own bitterness, and no one else can share its joy" (Proverbs 14:10).

The psalmist, David, was well aware of the state of his heart: "For I am poor and needy, and my heart is wounded within me" (Psalm 109:22). Are we as insightful as David about the state of our own heart? Do we acknowledge its condition either to ourselves or to God? Do we put on a mask, hiding our true self even from ourselves? Oblivious to our true state, we may continue to live out our lives unclear why we act and react the way we do.

Do you feel as though you have walked a well-trodden path, criss-crossing the wilderness without getting any nearer the Promised Land? Perhaps it is time to rest awhile and develop your relationship with Jesus. Let him explore your heart motivation, not to condemn but to transform and finally equip you for life in the land. Because this land involves warfare as well as blessing, a stout and fully committed heart is necessary.

Is Your Heart Too Frail To Respond To God?

For me, the autumn of 1994 heralded a rapid decline into depression. In the early days of the illness, I was quite unaware of my true state. All I knew was that everything was an effort, I felt increasingly distant from life around me, and tears seemed to be my ever-present companion. Sunday services had become torturous. They were too loud, too crowded, and, quite frankly, too full of life. I had taken to sitting near the door and leaving when it became too overwhelming to remain.

I hadn't sung for many weeks, but during the worship on one particular morning, God came alongside. I was asking him yet again, *Am I in sin because I cannot praise you? Show me my sin so I can confess and be restored.*

Immediately, I could "see" a shrivelled heart that, to an untrained eye, appeared lifeless. It was tiny and wrinkled – and it was mine. As I looked, God asked me, *How can you sing with gusto when your heart is barely beating?* In an instant, my loving Father made sense of everything I had been feeling for weeks.

Not content with offering understanding, God then "showed" me an index finger gently beginning to massage the heart. God was saying, *I'll keep you alive.* I couldn't have endured God's hand on my heart – it would have been too big and would have caused damage – but his index finger applied enough pressure to ensure life. I hadn't enough strength to worship God in an obvious sense through singing, but thanks to his life-giving touch, my worship that day consisted of staying in the same room as everybody else.

How strong is your heart right now? Perhaps it needs God's tender massage to nurture it back to health.

The Fortress

You may have experienced Christian leadership in some form. Perhaps you have worked with those also addressing their homosexuality. Many women enter into ministry with a genuine desire to help others know Christ. In my experience, it is easy to fall into the trap of being so clued in to ministering to others that we overlook personal areas that need addressing. Before long, a crack appears between what we say and the personal application of truth. Although I have long since lost the source book, author John Ritchie offers some insight:

> In spiritual things it's not what we know but what we actually possess that enriches our souls. Theoretic knowledge apart from appropriating faith is of little value. To read the words, "Blessed with all spiritual blessings," in the book of God is one thing; to have these blessings as a matter of realization in the soul is another thing. The measure of our actual spiritual wealth is not what we see to be contained in the promises of God, but *what we get out of them from day to day*. [Emphasis mine]

Unfortunately, for many women trying to juggle work, ministry and perhaps even a family, our head and heart knowledge of God can be poles apart. We can almost pride ourselves on our knowledge about him, yet, often due to time constraint, remain fairly ignorant of his presence in the recesses of our life. Either through fear of what God may reveal, or of the pain that may be stored, or through general ignorance, our hearts can deceive us as to our proper condition.

As we see in the Scriptures, God invests heavily in our hearts. Do we show equal investment? Am I making sure that my heart is a fertile place for God to dwell?

In our ignorance, we may be warring against our own hearts. Our ears may not hear his voice; perhaps hidden sin is preventing us from responding to him, or our isolating pain may leave us feeling abandoned and in great need.

Walking In The Light

Sin thrives in the dark. We also know that failing to be honest with others and ourselves prevents experiencing an abundant life. To expose one's heart is frightening for many people. There are no guarantees that we won't experience further hurt and rejection. But continuing to operate in the dark ensures that our relationship with God and with others will be impaired. "If we claim to have fellowship with him yet walk in the darkness, we lie and do not live by the truth. But if we walk in the light, as he is in the light, we have fellowship with one another, and the blood of Jesus, his Son, purifies us from all sin" (1 John 1:6f).

God knows every aspect of our heart. It is time *we* did. Bravery is required to step out from the fig leaves of falsehood and allow the true self to emerge. Wanting to be acceptable to others must not prevent living in the fullness of our identity in Christ. Many women have spent years addressing their homosexuality and have been accepted in this identity as an "ex-gay". They may have been paraded as someone "changed by Christ". But, for many women, the "change process" appears not only to stall, but also to stagnate after a number of years, despite ongoing effort. The danger here is to hide behind a label and settle for acceptance.

Who wants to admit that they have "failed"? Not wanting

to be exposed (yet again!), many women have rejected vulnerability for fear of further hurt. While this is an understandable response, in so doing we starve ourselves of the love, nurture and protection offered by Jesus and others. Hiding in the shadows ensures a deepening sense of isolation and loss. However desperate our feelings, we cannot overlook the truth that a Christian walk is a walk of love: that is, receiving from the Father and offering to others. If, because of our sense of failure, we have condemned ourselves to shadow living, we will fail to receive sustenance. A starved heart becomes weakened. Unable to receive from God, we have nothing to offer others and ultimately become more isolated from friends, family and the body of Christ.

Please hear what I am saying. *A starving person will eat anything.* Our heart needs nourishment and we may return to activities we have long since left in an effort to find sustenance. "He who is full loathes honey, but to the hungry even what is bitter tastes sweet" (Proverbs 27:7).

Over the years, I have known a number of women who have returned to an active homosexual life. Privately, they admit that this is not God's best for them. Many are in turmoil regarding their actions. But a sense of loss, failure and loneliness, and the need for intimacy and a sense of belonging, have left them with such a deep void that they feel they have no alternative but to return to Egypt.

War Or Peace?

In the book of Joshua, we read that war needed to cease before the Hebrews could fully claim the promises of the land. For many women addressing their homosexual inclinations, an internal war needs to cease before we can live in peace with God and others. In order to achieve that peace I need to ask myself pertinent questions: *Is my life reflecting my true inheritance – that of being seated in the heavenlies with Christ? Or am I eking out a meagre existence in poverty of spirit because I'm living ignorant of God's whisper in my inmost being? Am I living truthfully and honestly before God and others?*

A heart at war cannot plan for the future. It can deal only with the present. Continual warfare is exhausting and will ultimately grind a person down until they are susceptible to a "fast-food fix". No one can promise an easy life in the short or medium term. But we need to take an eternal view. "Those who sow in tears *will reap* with songs of joy. He who goes out weeping, carrying seed to sow, *will return* with songs of joy, carrying sheaves with him" (Psalm 126:4–6, emphasis mine).

There is no resurrection without the passion. There is no joy without the cross. Our pilgrimage may consist of more ravines than summits, compared with others, but let the embrace of the Father and the words, "Well done, my good and faithful servant" be our spur to continue the walk. Let us address our heart, holding on to the promise found in Proverbs: "A heart at peace gives life to the body" (Proverbs 14:30).

A strong heart is required if we are to engage in pilgrimage. Hearts that are able to receive and retain God's love will remain strong irrespective of what lies ahead. They will pump divine life around our otherwise weary bodies, encouraging us to press on towards our goal. That godly love will refresh and encourage other pilgrims walking a similar journey. Out of an ongoing strength provided by our Lord, we will be able to minister out of abundance rather than need, and enjoy healthy companionship with our fellow travellers.

My Heart Journey

As for my heart, much has happened since 1994. Allowing God to shed his light and pour out his love into my heart has been uncomfortable, to say the least. Learning to live in tune with my heart has been, and still is, somewhat alien, but it is as I rest in God's presence that I experience the most benefit from this journey. My relationship with him is intimate and often joyful, and this closeness allows me to hear his voice, not only for myself, but also to help others in their discipleship. A depth and contentment is developing that is priceless, and I realise that my first love is becoming an ever-maturing love, capable of withstanding many storms.

Restoration

Two days ago, while working on this chapter, God gifted me with a precious 30 minutes. I felt compelled to walk away from the computer and kneel by the bed, where God began to speak to me.

The Lord gave me a picture of my heart that reminded me of the American Embassy in London. It was large and imposing, with a number of steep steps leading up to the building. As is currently the case, the front of the building had three-deep anti-terrorist concrete blocks and armed police protecting the inhabitants. The immediate street was cordoned off and there was no access for the public; even the traffic was subject to detour. I sensed that that was the protection I had engaged since the beginning of my illness, and that now the Lord wanted to do a new thing.

Although the building looked impenetrable, it was actually roofless and filled with a fiery, golden glow and a piercing white light. The interior was a place where I could have uninterrupted communion with the Lord, where I could rest, reflect, and be energised and strengthened by him. From that position of well-being, I could minister without fear of being shredded or discarded or weakened. My heart was abiding, and will abide, in him.

Action, however, was required on my part. I had to remove the armed police and the concrete anti-terrorist barriers, sweep the steps clean and invite people to come up to what seemed like a colonnade encircling the house.

The rest of the given word is irrelevant to this chapter, but I now know that the *major* restoration work on my heart has been completed. Strengthened from within, I can now live with an unguarded heart towards Jesus and minister with his love and compassion.

A heart that beats in time with Jesus enables the believer to share in his life at a more fundamental level. One may imagine the pleasure of ministering in his name and under his anointing, but to mirror Jesus means to expose the weakness of self so that all glory and honour and worship are directed towards the Father. I hadn't long been a Christian before I found out that I don't "do" weak!

Chapter Five

Wonderful Weakness

"Let the weak say I am strong,
Let the poor say I am rich,
Let the blind say I can see,
It's what the Lord has done in me." [10]

God's Chosen People

Set apart, protected, and guided since the time of Abraham, the Hebrews knew that they were God's chosen people. Provided that they remained faithful to their Maker, the Hebrews understood that their future was secure in the Promised Land. Having been taught the ways of God during their travels in the wilderness, and despite the presence of Canaanite enemies, God's people could be confident of success.

Like them, we too are God's chosen people. Moments prior to my conversion, I read John 15:16: "You did not choose me, but I chose you and appointed you to go and bear fruit – fruit that will last." To be chosen, especially by God, fed my rather tenuous sense of worth. I had spent years focusing on what I could achieve rather than on who I was, and my interpretation of this scripture fed into the action-led part of me. *I am able,* I concluded, *therefore I am chosen.* The passage in 1 Peter merely fed into this belief: "But you are a chosen people, a royal priesthood, a holy nation, a people belonging to

---

10. Reuben Morgan, "Let the Weak Say I am Strong", Hillsong Publishing/ Kingsway's Thankyou Music, Eastbourne, 1998.

God, that you may declare the praises of him who called you out of darkness into his wonderful light" (1 Peter 2:9).

Buoyed by such verses, I was ready to take on the "heathen world"! But the Bible has a glorious habit of building you up and giving you a holy kick in the stomach at the same time. Reading 1 Corinthians 1:26–29, days later, burst my bubble of confidence and offended me to the core: "[Sisters], think of what you were when you were called. Not many of you were wise by human standards; not many were influential; not many were of noble birth. But God chose the foolish things of the world to shame the wise; God chose the weak things of the world to shame the strong. He chose the lowly things of this world and the despised things – and the things that are not – to nullify the things that are, so that no one may boast before him" (1 Corinthians 1:26–29).

But I didn't want to be associated with these Corinthians! Who was God calling weak? Didn't he know I was a high flyer intent on shinning up the ladder of success? Didn't Paul realise that "I can do everything through *me* who gives me strength" (adapted from Philippians 4:13)? I was well entrenched in the Olympian ideal of "higher, faster, stronger" which now permeates Western society. I had much to learn.

Pride

Confidence in self, no matter how able we are, or from whatever faulty premise we begin, is the greatest barrier to faith in God. The above passage confronts our pride because we, like the Hebrews, are chosen not because of what we can offer, but because of God's mercy. We are chosen not because of what we can do, but because of what we *can't* do. We can't save ourselves from eternal damnation: we are in need of a Saviour.

The world system places emphasis on our ability, but God is more concerned with our availability. The apostle Paul had much to offer. A well-educated Hebrew scholar and Roman citizen, and a high-ranking official with far-reaching authority, Saul, as he was then known, was obviously highly motivated and committed to his cause. In a worldly sense he was to be admired, and Paul must have taken great pride in his well-earned position. But Paul's strengths were a hindrance to God's purposes for him, and years of discipleship were required before Paul was able to state that he counted *everything* as loss compared to knowing Christ (Philippians 3:7–9). It was the apostle's humility rather than his ability that deepened his relationship with, and his usefulness to, God.

From Desperation To Acceptance And Delight

> To keep me from becoming conceited because of these surpassingly great revelations, there was given me a thorn in my flesh, a messenger of Satan, to torment me. Three times I pleaded with the Lord to take it away from me. But he said to me, "My grace is sufficient for you, for my power is made perfect in weakness." Therefore I will boast all the more gladly about my weaknesses, so that Christ's power may rest on me. That is why, for Christ's sake, I delight in weaknesses, in insults, in hardships, in persecutions, in difficulties. For when I am weak, then I am strong. (2 Corinthians 12:7–10)

Paul is gloriously vague in the above passage. Refraining from naming his particular thorn allows each reader to identify with the difficulties he faced. When times are particularly tough, I almost envy Paul, for he mentions a mere thorn, whereas I feel as though the whole bush is gouging me in the side!

There is much to be taken from these verses, but I want to focus on three obvious stages.

Ask God to remove the weakness

I had a friend, Richard, who was a 60-a-day man. Wherever he went, a cloud of yellowy smoke followed. The car, the van and his desk were littered with discarded packets of cigarettes and money-off coupons; Richard didn't buy his fags by the packet, but by the car load, as he undertook frequent duty-free trips to France.

One day, not long after he recommitted his life to the Lord, Richard prayed a very simple prayer that God would remove his addiction to nicotine and take away the desire to smoke. I admit that I said the required "Amen" without a modicum of faith. After all, I had heard and made so many similar prayers over the years without success that I had become resigned to "failure".

But, from that moment twelve years ago, Richard has not smoked a single cigarette. Moreover, he didn't suffer nicotine withdrawal or any other side effect that is linked with smoking.

A word from God

This is where life can begin to unravel if we are only ever geared up to God answering in the affirmative. Have you prayed similar prayers to Richard's regarding your homosexual struggles? Over the years, has your faith waned as God appears to be ignoring your request, and do you now pray in a "faith-free zone"? It is true that Richard's prayer was answered by God in a dramatic, life-changing way regarding his smoking addiction, but he would be the first to admit that there are many other important issues he has to address, and has addressed, without God's miraculous intervention.

Pouting, moaning and claiming that life isn't fair will not bring any of us closer to God. Praying for a "more normal" problem in exchange for your current struggles won't bring success either. God doesn't do trade-ins! And hoping that he'll succumb to your manipulative whine, *I thought you loved me*, shows a complete lack of respect and understanding. " 'For my thoughts are not your thoughts, neither are your ways my ways,' declares the Lord" (Isaiah 55:8). In 2 Corinthians 12:8 the apostle Paul says that he pleaded with God to take this thorn away. God's word to him was succinct: "My grace is sufficient for you, for my power is made perfect in weakness" (2 Corinthians 12:9).

Are you prepared to hear the same answer? Having spent years addressing lesbian thought patterns and behaviours, and developing your spiritual life in the hope that your homosexual orientation will become a thing of the past, are you now ready to live with this weakness? Do you have the courage to fall on God's grace and live in the midst of your struggles in order for his power to be revealed? Instead of seeking to remove your weakness, are you prepared to offer it as part of your living sacrifice? Are you able to embrace this part of you, not to satisfy yourself, but to serve God?

This is a big call.

Kingdom purposes

"Therefore I will boast all the more gladly about my weaknesses, so that Christ's power may rest on me. That is why, for Christ's sake, I delight in weaknesses, in insults, in hardships, in persecutions, in difficulties. For when I am weak, then I am strong" (2 Corinthians 12:9b, 10).

Paul here is laying down his life for the sake of the kingdom. He is prepared to face death every day in order that the life of God may be revealed. The British preacher Ken

McGreavy points out that it is not our circumstances that determine our fruitfulness, but our attitude to the circumstances. Paul could have heard God's answer and railed against it for the rest of his life, becoming gradually more bitter in attitude and fruitless in ministry. But, in laying down his desire for healing or change, Paul was able to take up God's purposes, thus propelling him into further kingdom work. The ever-present thorn, whatever it was, kept the apostle dependent on his Lord and effective in service.

Shame Or Delight?

It seems perverse to delight in one's weakness. Surely our frailties are shameful things, to be concealed at all costs? Revealing the chinks in our armour lays our most sensitive parts open to ridicule and attack. Who wants to live in an exposed place where we may get hurt? The natural inclination to protect ourselves dictates that we conceal all weak areas and reveal only our strengths. I present my acceptable face to you so that, irrespective of my inner fear of rejection, you will consider me worthwhile and accept me into your life.

Do I want you to know that I can understand and explain the word of God, or that I struggle with issues of sexuality, experience mental health problems, and daily face the difficulties of addiction?

Do we think more or less of people when they admit their failures? A couple of years ago, Estelle Morris, then Minister of Education in the United Kingdom, resigned. Following a lengthy period of bad press and complaints from those in education, Ms Morris handed in her notice, admitting that she wasn't good enough to remain in office. With one sentence Morris stunned and disarmed her critics. They were amazed by her honesty. No one in politics ever admitted they weren't good enough for the job. Her candid self-appraisal exhibited such integrity in the usually fallen world of politics that Morris's opinion was sought far more after her resignation than it ever was while she held office!

Would a more honest statement on the issues we *all* face as Christians bring greater glory to God than the hollow ring of victory so often yelled, although rarely exhibited, from the church congregation?

Honesty and integrity in the pilgrim's struggle towards God will speak volumes to men and women seeking a path through this often difficult existence, and may help them join the worthwhile journey to life.

What I Really Really Want

The truth is that I don't want God's grace to comfort me when I am weak. I don't want God's strength to keep me going when I am facing particular issues. I don't want him to tell me I am "the apple of his eye" when I struggle with rejection. Why? *Because I don't want the weaknesses in the first place.* I want healing. I want to be an overcomer. I want to be victorious. I want to be a strong Christian, striding through life preaching God's word and claiming God's kingdom wherever I go: I don't want to be in need.

But if I act on those thoughts, I am storing up major problems. If I ignore or paper over my weaknesses, I am, in effect, rejecting God's offer of grace and strength. I am saying, "Let me be a Christian on my terms and in my strength." I am heading for disaster.

God's Way

However invasive or benign your homosexual difficulties are right now, I encourage you to side with the apostle Paul: "If I must boast, I will boast of the things that show my weakness" (2 Corinthians 11:30). In so doing we open the door to God's power being manifest in our life. Do you seek the greater gifts to serve and bless God's kingdom? Then live as an alien in this world and do not conform to its ways, but "be transformed by the renewing of your mind" (Romans 12:2a). Do you think as the world does, and live in shame regarding your weakness? Or, like Paul, do you see those flaws as an opportunity to serve God more powerfully?

Living In Weakness

Choosing to live from a point of need promotes dependency on God. We may think that a change in orientation and desire may be good for us, and indeed it may, but God is not concerned with what is *good*; he wants the *best* for us. Experiencing a change in orientation, falling in love with a man, marrying and having children may well be good for us in the temporal, but not changing our basic orientation or healing us from all of our weaknesses may *be in our eternal best interests*.

For Paul, his ongoing frailty, his thorn, prevented him from becoming conceited. God's call on his life, to bring the gospel to the Gentile world, was immense, and the temptation to see himself as superior to others must have been great. But Paul was able to capture God's thinking regarding his Achilles heel, and choosing to see this thorn with an eternal perspective enabled Paul genuinely to delight in his weakness. Why? Because it promoted his relationship with Jesus and released him into further ministry.

Do you see your homosexual weakness and temptation towards sin as a stumbling block keeping you from God, or a stepping stone towards greater intimacy with Jesus?

Despise, Withhold, Or Offer?

"Therefore, I urge you, [sisters], in view of God's mercy, to offer your bodies as living sacrifices, holy and pleasing to God – this is your spiritual act of worship. Do not conform any longer to the pattern of this world, but be transformed by the renewing of your mind. Then you will be able to test and approve what God's will is – his good, pleasing and perfect will" (Romans 12:1f).

I have spent most of my Christian life despising my homosexual tendencies and seeing them as a real problem. Having done all that I could to rid myself of them, I then subconsciously withheld all desires, longings and temptations from God and no longer "bothered" him with that aspect of my life. Ashamed of my failure to "progress" to the next stage of healing (becoming attracted to men in a romantic way), I chose to ignore my sexuality altogether. In effect, I closed down and became asexual in outlook; I disowned and excluded the unchanged and partially changed aspects of my life, and concentrated on the positive attributes that, in my mind, would be useful to the kingdom. I offered God my strengths and gifts in service. Not surprisingly, suppressing such a large part of me helped to plunge my life into the darkness of depression.

But the beginning of Romans 12 refers to *my whole body*, my mind, my desires, my emotions, and my weaknesses as well as my strengths. My act of worship means offering up that shameful, hidden, "failed" part of me, as well as those strengths and gifts of which I am so proud.

> I will offer up my life in spirit and truth,
> Pouring out the oil of love as my worship to You.
> In surrender I must give my every part;
> Lord, receive the sacrifice of a broken heart.[11]

When you sing that chorus or something similar, are you offering only your strengths and gifts? Are you able to offer your homosexual orientation, your wayward desires and your secret longings to Jesus? Do we willingly lie on the altar on a daily basis, offering him all of us, the unchanged as well as the changed? Can we, like Paul, delight in our weaknesses, knowing that God will lovingly accept and transform them into kingdom gifts?

Living In Weakness

> Your attitude should be the same as that of Christ Jesus:

> Who, being in very nature God,
> did not consider equality with God
> something to be grasped,
> but made himself nothing,
> taking the very nature of a servant,
> being made in human likeness.
> And being found in appearance as a man,
> he humbled himself
> and became obedient to death – even death on a cross!
>
> (Philippians 2:5–8)

---

11. Matt Redman, "I will offer up my life", Kingsway's Thankyou Music, Eastbourne, 1994.

Jesus lived out of the weakness of his humanity rather than the strength of his deity. He was the ultimate high priest who suffered rejection, humiliation and finally a painful death so that God's purpose, reconciliation with humankind, would be fulfilled. If Jesus had lived out of his strengths, we would still be awaiting a saviour. If Paul had lived out of his strengths, the gospel would not have spread beyond the Jewish nation. And if we persist in living out of our strengths, we will prevent God's power from being made manifest in us.

The First Commandment

"Hear, O Israel: The Lord our God, the Lord is one. Love the Lord your God with all your heart and with all your soul and with all your strength" (Deuteronomy 6:4).

The emphasis here is on the word "all". If I cannot worship God with the weakest part of me, then I cannot fulfil the first commandment. It is not enough to offer him the parts I find acceptable, but I must offer all my heart, all my soul, and all my strength. If my life is truly dedicated to him I need to offer:

- the foolish part of me that goes my own rebellious way
- the weak, addictive part of my personality that tends towards worship of the created rather than the Creator
- the lowly, shameful parts of my personality that are considered too unworthy to expose
- those attractions and desires that bombard my idle moments.

This form of worship is not the "happy-clappy" sort often experienced on a Sunday morning, but worship offered when we choose to stand in the light rather than lurk in the shadows of Christian life. In exposing the hidden, we are offering an act of worship that is wholly acceptable to God. This vulnerability comes with a promise: "Then you will be able to test and approve what God's will is – his good, pleasing and perfect will" (Romans 12:2b).

Do you want to dwell in the Promised Land? Do you want to know and fulfil God's purposes? Then, like Paul, delight in your weakness, and offer your homosexuality as a wonderful, spiritual act of worship.

Get To Know God

How did Paul reach this incredible position? He made his relationship with God central to his life, and we have the opportunity to do the same. Spending time in God's company, reading his word and applying his teaching to our life creates an opportunity for deep relationship with him. As we learn of God's character, marvel at his ways, and gaze upon perfection, our own imperfections will be exposed. Like Isaiah, we will recognise the gulf between self and God (Isaiah 6:5), and, like Paul, we will be tempted to cry out, "What a wretched man I am! Who will rescue me from this body of death?" (Romans 7:24). There are no short cuts to discipleship, but, even if it takes years to learn, we will eventually realise that we are but dust (Psalm 103), and our good deeds are like filthy rags (Isaiah 64:6). Ultimately, we will stop trying to operate in our own strength and come to realise that our weaknesses are a vital part of the self.

As we bring them to the fore, we give Jesus full rein to minister to us. He came to preach the good news to those who knew they were weak in spirit, to heal those who knew their hearts were damaged and in need of love, to declare freedom to those bound by addictions, relational problems and loneliness. He wants to bring sight to those who are spiritually blind. If we don't offer our weaknesses to Jesus, how can he walk with us in our loneliness, fill up the emptiness within or comfort us in our distress?

It is risky to expose the hidden weaknesses. But in exposing them to Jesus and to one another, we give opportunity to Jesus to transform them into areas of strength.

> Blessed are those whose strength is in you,
> Who have set their hearts on pilgrimage.
> As they pass through the Valley of Baca [trouble],
> They make it a place of springs.   (Psalm 84:5)

Successful pilgrimage requires finding our strength in God, being guided by God, and pursuing God above all else.

When I think of weaknesses common to all, I can't help considering the issue of emotional dependency. Led by seemingly unrelenting inner needs, it is all too easy for women to look to the readily available for the immediate feel-good factor. The next chapter will look at this recurrent problem.

Chapter Six

The Interruption
Of Friendship

"But this deeply satisfying friendship became the road to my anguish, because soon I discovered that the enormous space that had been opened for me could not be filled by the one who had opened it. I became possessive, needy, and dependent, and when the friendship finally had to be interrupted, I fell apart. I felt abandoned, rejected, and betrayed. Indeed, the extremes touched each other."[12]

Insidious Dependency

In my book, *Out of Egypt: Leaving Lesbianism Behind*,[13] an entire chapter addressed the issue of emotional dependency. But, like a perennial weed with a long taproot, the inclination to dependency has a habit of returning! And like the persistent dandelion spoiling an otherwise lovely lawn, emotional dependency requires the gardener's special attention.

I am thankful for Nouwen's book, *The Inner Voice of Love*, from which the above quote is taken. Over the years I have found his outlook on life to be most helpful and worthy of great consideration. This chapter is based on thoughts that have arisen from reading and studying *The Inner Voice of Love* over a period of time.

---

12. Henri J M Nouwen, *The Inner Voice of Love* (Image Books, New York, 1998), page XV.
13. Jeanette Howard, *Out of Egypt: Leaving Lesbianism Behind* (Monarch Books, London, 1993).

Another Fine Mess

I rather enjoy watching the old Laurel and Hardy films. At some point in every movie, the title and subject matter being irrelevant, Oliver Hardy always turns on his companion, Stan Laurel, blaming him for their current disaster-ridden predicament. He shouts, hits out and generally stomps around, absolving himself from any guilt. Predictably, Stan Laurel pulls a face, shrugs his shoulders, points in various directions and whimpers, implying he has no idea how it all happened.

When it comes to emotional dependency, we can adopt either of the two roles. The mess, however bad, always seems a little easier to bear if we are able to lay the blame at someone else's feet. Sadly, even if we, like Laurel, are clueless as to its origins, dependency, irrespective of whoever else is involved, is definitely a mess we have "gotten" ourselves into!

Teasing Out The Problem

Jenny and Pippa were friends who roomed together throughout college. They both led active social lives, although, according to Jenny, Pippa was always the more gregarious and risk-taking of the two. To her credit, although never short of invitations out, Pippa always found time to make sure Jenny was OK.

"That was the amazing thing about her," mused Jenny. "Nothing was ever too much effort for Pippa. She always seemed genuinely pleased to be in my company, she affirmed me in all kinds of small ways, appreciated my outlook on life, my Christian maturity, and was always ready to give a supportive hug or touch."

"Sounds a bit too good to be true," I ventured. We were

walking the dogs on one of the many footpaths near the South Downs. It was a glorious day and Jenny was in a reflective mood.

"That's the point," she said. "When I first started rooming with her, Pippa annoyed me more than anything else. Although she would ask my opinion about something, I was left in no doubt which one of us would make the ultimate decision. She was fun to be with, but there never seemed to be an "off" button, and some days I was quite exhausted in her company. Through Pippa I got to know many of the other students quite quickly, which was great, but the ever-open-door policy became quite trying, especially when various college assignments were due. I'm not sure how I changed from being an irritated room mate to a dependent friend in the space of two months!"

Reality To Idealisation

I had certainly come across something similar in my own life. When we view a person in their entirety, we are aware of their less appealing qualities as well as their more pleasant ones. That is a normal way of relating. For instance, your friend may be a wonderful listener in general, but you know not to approach her until that first cup of coffee has hit the mark. Or she may always prove to be great company once you have forgiven her, yet again, for arriving 30 minutes after the agreed time. A healthy friendship sees the other person as a multifaceted "package".

In my experience, dependency can arise once you *lose that broad view*. The progression into dependency appears as follows:

- You are fully *aware and accepting* of the friend's faults and virtues. Communication is good, so, at times, you can voice your frustration regarding her persistent tardiness and have no problem when she points out her irritations. You appreciate getting together when you can and are confident in the strength of the friendship irrespective of the time spent in each other's company.

- You consistently choose to *overlook those irritations* because you don't want to upset your friend in any way, and you yourself want to be seen by her in the best light: all-accommodating and loving.

- Rather than merely overlooking her foibles, you *continually excuse them* in your mind, offering quite acceptable reasons for her bad behaviour or inconsiderate comments. It is becoming necessary for you to see your friend only in a positive light. You are mentally moulding the friend into someone who can most satisfy your requirements.

- There are *no flaws* in your friend. Everything she does is right and everything she says is perfectly acceptable. You no longer see her as a three-dimensional figure but as someone who has only positive qualities.

- Even that view diminishes and you end up noticing only those attributes that *best serve you*. She is your "need-meeter" rather than your friend.

Talking with Jenny helped me understand the process. Pippa's positive qualities – her friendly affirming nature, caring tactile approach, and genuine appreciation of her room mate – exposed Jenny's neediness. Consider the scenario: a student, first time away from home, shy and with few friends.

Add to that Jenny's long-held low self-esteem and longing to feel accepted and cared for by someone whom she genuinely likes. The situation was ripe for dependency. To be friends with someone who was also popular with fellow students was just icing on the cake.

Trade-off

Living with exposed needs was too painful to contemplate. Jenny's ever-demanding "requirements" of affirmation, care, touch and appreciation had to be either reburied or met in some way. Although she didn't recognise the thought process at the time, Jenny had subconsciously made an important decision: her deep-seated needs could be met only if she spent most of her time in Pippa's company. A trade-off was required.

Jenny would have to overlook those characteristics of Pippa that annoyed her and she would also have to give up her right to decision-making, privacy, and peaceful contemplation within the flat. To challenge Pippa would, in Jenny's distorted view, risk losing the friendship – an altogether unacceptable thought. Although Pippa was probably unaware of the unfolding scene, Jenny created a false environment and an unbalanced friendship in order to satisfy the gnawing hunger created by a previously unmet need for love, acceptance, affirmation, and company.

In truth, the real Jenny got lost in the unreal and ultimately untenable friendship.

In the early days, of course, Jenny was oblivious to such details. In her estimation, life had never been better.

Insatiable Need

Like a drug habit that needs an ever-increasing fix, an emotionally dependent relationship requires continual feeding. You need more time, more attention, more touch, to feel as good as you once felt in your friend's company. But the need is like a black hole whose size is unfathomable and can never be filled through one friendship.

Pippa's fine qualities highlighted Jenny's needs, but could not, and never were, intended to meet them.

The Pursuit Of Being Fully Loved

When I consider the numerous dependent relationships in which I have engaged, I wonder how much of myself I have traded in order to feel fully loved. How much of the other person have I sought, stolen and stockpiled, vainly hoping that that will be the bit of love that will satisfy? How much have I given away in the emotional, physical and spiritual arena? How much of my affection has been returned as an unopened and rejected present? How much has been returned used, damaged and seemingly beyond repair? What parts of me were thrown to the ground and trampled beneath angry feet?

What about you? At what point will you stop ripping off those tender parts of yourself and offering them to others as barter? What price are you willing to pay in order to feel love?

"A lot of giving and receiving has a violent quality, because the givers and receivers act more out of need than out of trust. What looks like generosity is actually manipulation, and what looks like love is really a cry for affection or support."[14] When will we stop looking to the imperfect, vainly

---

14. Henri J M Nouwen, *The Inner Voice of Love* (Image Books, New York, 1998), page 66.

hoping that they will fill up all the empty holes and make everything all right?

Returning To Gilgal

Joshua chapter four recounts the miraculous parting of the River Jordan, thus establishing Joshua's leadership in the minds of the Israelites. Having crossed safely on dry land, the people set up their first camp at Gilgal. Situated a mere two miles from the stronghold of Jericho, Gilgal became the centre of worship and government during the invasion of Canaan.

The Ark of the Covenant resided there and a memorial of twelve stones was erected to remind future generations of God's faithfulness. At Gilgal, the Israelites renewed their covenant to God, and, in full view of their enemies, all 40,000 fighting men were circumcised, thus proving that despite being rendered incapable of personal protection, the men, their families and their possessions could dwell safely under God's protection. By disarming the troops in full view of the enemy, God made it clear that strength would not be found in their own ability or methods, but in the provision, timing and protection of the Lord.

After the circumcision, Passover was celebrated for the first time in 39 years, and later a commander of the Lord's army presented himself to Joshua.

Designated as the rallying point and debriefing site for the troops, a place of worship, and a secure place for rest and renewal for all God's people, Gilgal was an important but sadly overlooked and underused Israelite base camp.

Do you have a Gilgal? Is there a place where you can lay yourself open before God, knowing that he will protect and care for you? Do you daily set out from Gilgal refreshed and renewed, and return for debriefing, sustenance and relaxation? Do you meet with God on a daily basis? Do you know his purpose and plan for your life? Do you know that he longs to sit with you and delight in your company? Are you able to agree with the psalmist:

> You prepare a table before me
> in the presence of my enemies.
> You anoint my head with oil;
> my cup overflows.
>
> (Psalm 23:5)

Are you living out of a place of abundance or need?

Serial Dependency

Our tendency to engage in serial dependency should ring internal alarm bells. We can continue on this faulty path, interrupting and possibly even destroying potentially life-enhancing friendships, or we can sit in a safe place with our Lord and address the presenting problems. Perhaps you used to have an excellent base camp where you met regularly with your Lord, and out of that place of security and empowerment your Christian walk was strong and your ministry powerful. Life with Jesus was vibrant and joyful, enriching and exciting; you challenged strongholds and saw powers and principalities crumble before your Warrior King. And now? Has the warfare proved too hard and too long? Do the rewards seem too distant? Have you become weary in your struggle against sin? Do you need renewing, strengthening, envisioning? Have you wandered away from Gilgal and are you now pursuing other locations and/or people to meet those very real needs?

Return to Gilgal. Return to the presence of our Lord. Lay down your heavy burden and rest in the security of his encampment. Yes, Gilgal is located within the enemy's reach, but it is there where you will find everything you need for life. In that place we can all safely admit our inner weaknesses and seek strength in God. He will restore 20/20 vision and equip us for the battles we have yet to encounter. In going to him with our needs we allow God to renew us.

Receiving And Retaining God's Love

Receiving and *retaining* God's love is paramount if we are to break this cycle of dependency. We may be adept at receiving God's love through his word, worship and the fellowship of other believers, but is our retention of that love poor? Does God's love haemorrhage out of as yet unhealed raw wounds of rejection, loss or grief? How do I know if my heart is a bowl retaining and overflowing with God's love, or a sieve that allows his love to gush through as fast as it is poured in?

A useful indicator can be found in one's service to others. When you give in the hope of return you are giving out of a position of need and not of plenty. If you do not operate out of a bowl-shaped heart filled with God's love, you serve with a sieve-like heart. That flawed service will have a hidden agenda demanding that this designated person help block some of your heart holes and pour their love, appreciation and care into your needy cavern. But if that is your *modus operandi*, you are embarking on a course doomed to failure: "Only God can fully dwell in that deepest place in you and give you a sense of safety. But the danger remains that you will let other people run away with your sacred center thus throwing you into anguish."[15]

---

15. Ibid., page 71.

Listen Only To The Voice Of Love

Hanging on to and living out of God's thoughts towards me is the only way I can experience and retain his love. His love is pure and truthful; he *is* love. The thoughts I labour under regarding myself are wayward at best, and other people's thoughts towards me vary, but God's thoughts towards me are always loving and constant.

> He reached down from on high and took hold of me;
> he drew me out of deep waters.
> He rescued me from my powerful enemy,
> from my foes, who were too strong for me.
> They confronted me in the day of my disaster,
> but the Lord was my support.
> He brought me out into a spacious place;
> he rescued me because he delighted in me.
>
> (Psalm 18:16–19)

"How great is the love the Father has lavished on us, that we should be called children of God! And that is what we are!" (1 John 3:1a). "In love he predestined us to be adopted as his sons through Jesus Christ, in accordance with his pleasure and will – to the praise of his glorious grace, which he has freely given us in the One he loves. In him we have redemption through his blood, the forgiveness of sins, in accordance with the riches of God's grace that he lavished on us with all wisdom and understanding" (Ephesians 1:4b–8).

I can listen to his voice and act upon his unfailing love, or look for love in all the wrong places. The choice is mine. But at what point will I allow Jesus to be the rock he says he is, my shield, my defender, and my ever-present help in times of need? At what point will I allow him to demonstrate just who he is: my sufficiency and my all in all? In all the running around and chasing after temporary respite, listening only to the jarring words offered by fellow travellers, will I ever stop long enough to hear his gentle whisper, "Be still, and know that I am God"?

At Gilgal I can remove my armour of self-protection. At Gilgal I can sit and be ministered to by his angels, and I can delight myself in God's all-restoring presence. At Gilgal God can heal my wounds, fill those empty holes and strengthen me in the core of my being.

Delighting In Dependency?

As I mentioned in the previous chapter, "Wonderful Weakness", our attitude towards the difficulties we face is extremely important. A fear of, and hatred towards, the weakness of dependency can paralyse us into never seeking friendships, or, through shame, drive dependency issues underground where they will continue to grow and strengthen in power.

I have an inclination towards dependent relationships; pretending otherwise sets me up for failure. But when temptation is strong, or I am feeling weak, it is imperative to return to Gilgal, to God's presence. It is only there, after I have confessed my sin of idolatry and need for God, that I can hope to address my wayward emotions. Admitting to the weakness without shame, in the knowledge that God's strength will be sufficient, brings comfort. To be accountable to others and invest in different friendships helps offset potential emotional storms and helps reset my course to the ways of God. At Gilgal, God not only reveals himself but also uncovers areas of me that require his touch.

The Balance Of Friendship

Henri Nouwen's book *The Inner Voice of Love* results from a journal he kept during a difficult period when he was forced to question his source of affirmation, love and acceptance. The following quote is taken from late on in the book: "Many of your friendships grew from your need for affection, affirmation, and emotional support. But now you must seek friends to whom you can relate from your center, from the place where you know that you are deeply loved. Then you can be with others in a non-possessive way. Real friends find their inner correspondence where both know the love of God. There spirit speaks to spirit and heart to heart."[16]

Not depending on our friends to mend our sieve-like heart frees both parties to come and go in complete freedom. One friend may be capable of offering great love wrapped in grand gestures; another may offer the gentle touch of an arm. When our heart is operating out of a place of fullness, we can accept both gestures with equal gratitude. Although we will certainly have preferences, we do not *need* one more than the other. We can allow our friends to express themselves when and according to how *they* feel, rather than demanding a particular response.

Operating out of a position of relative wholeness allows us to stand during all other struggles we may have to face. Standing in the knowledge of God's love, rather than collapsing under the weight of our own need, brings many benefits. Opportunity is provided to hear the voice of God through many people and to see beyond the immediate and catch a glimpse of eternity. We can offer a voice to help guide others on a similar journey, and from a standing position our arms

16. Ibid., page 80.

are free to reach out and embrace, and our feet free to walk to or from others, during difficult times.

The Danger Of Distraction

Vacuuming and dusting the house are not listed among my favourite things to do. But, over the past few weeks, it is amazing how often I have welcomed the opportunity to clean rather than sit at my computer and write. The beautiful countryside just outside the window calls, the kettle beckons from the kitchen, and the fridge positively yells for my attention! Such is the danger of distraction.

I am not a mother, but I spent a year living with a young couple and their son, Sam. I soon learned the art of distracting the child from its source of grievance. Kissing, cuddling or getting excited over a favourite toy proved successful, provided there was no particular reason for the tears. But if there *was* a specific reason, like hunger, or colic, or a full nappy, the grizzling would return with ever-increasing intensity. Something concrete had to be done.

Similarly, if we merely distract ourselves from the issues that need addressing, then pain and discomfort will return. Without exposing our need and allowing the healing hand of God to touch that rawness, *the dependency cycle will continue*. Distraction can be great fun, but I have still had to sit down at the computer, Sam's nappy still had to be changed, and your empty heart holes still need to be filled with God's love.

Chapter Seven

Know Your Enemy, Know Your Boundaries

"If you know the enemy and know yourself you need not fear the result of a hundred battles."

Sun Tzu, *The Art of War*

Preparation For War

Remember how the Lord your God led you all the way in the desert these forty years, to humble you and to test you in order to know what was in your heart, whether or not you would keep his commands. He humbled you, causing you to hunger and then feeding you with manna, which neither you nor your fathers had known, to teach you that man does not live on bread alone but on every word that comes from the mouth of the Lord. Your clothes did not wear out and your feet did not swell during these forty years. Know then in your heart that as a man disciplines his son, so the Lord your God disciplines you. (Deuteronomy 8:2–5)

When a young man or woman joins the armed forces, they do not have their sights set on the immediate twelve-week basic training, but on a career that may involve the next 30 years of their life. The initial twelve weeks of hard graft are necessary to sift out the men and women who are committed to the cause from those who lack the required dedication. The drop-out rate among new recruits is high as they are tested in such areas as discipline, fitness, and aptitude. Training doesn't end after the three-month period, but becomes more specialised as the individual takes on and refines certain military skills. Such intense training is necessary. When patrolling the streets of Iraq or another world hot spot, the soldier needs confidence in the skill and dedication not only of himself, but also of his fellow combatants.

All Christians are required to walk in the wilderness. For some it is akin to the intensity of the twelve-week basic training; for others, a refinement of their current walk. Unlike the Hebrews of old whom God tried to keep in the Promised Land, we will be led into the wilderness for periods of time as part of our discipleship. It is not, therefore, something to fear or consider as personal failure (unless our sin has taken us into the desert), but as something to welcome. Times in the wilderness vary. How willing we are to lay down our self-determination, reliance on our natural abilities, and wilful heart rebellion will determine the length of walk. Make no mistake: God will do everything he can to weaken our confidence in self so that we will trust fully in him. Submitting our heart, mind, soul and body to God is a prerequisite for dwelling in the Promised Land.

Who Is The Enemy?

> When the Lord your God brings you into the land you are entering to possess and drives out before you many nations – the Hittites, Girgashites, Amorites, Canaanites, Perizzites, Hivites and Jebusites, seven nations larger and stronger than you – and when the Lord your God has delivered them over to you and you have defeated them, then you must destroy them totally. Make no treaty with them, and show them no mercy. (Deuteronomy 7:1f)

Who are these people singled out by Moses? They must be more than mere names that make the spellcheck on my computer see red!

Many Christians have difficulty with the Old Testament because they read of God's propensity towards the annihilation of any nation that is in opposition to Israel. It doesn't sit too well with their understanding of an all-loving God. Such thinking reflects an ignorance of God's character. God is holy and righteous and cannot look upon, or entertain, sin, and the Bible makes it clear that God's action towards the various nations does not signify that the Hebrews possessed an inherent moral superiority.

> After the Lord your God has driven them out before you, do not say to yourself, "The Lord has brought me here to take possession of this land because of my righteousness." No, it is on account of the wickedness of these nations that the Lord is going to drive them out before you. It is not because of your righteousness or your integrity that you are going in to take possession of their land; but on account of the wickedness of these nations. (Deuteronomy 9:4–5b)

Indeed, further reading of God's word shows that he destroys the Hebrews for their wickedness with equal alacrity! The history of the nations listed in Deuteronomy chapter seven shows their continued rebellion towards him and their direct opposition to all that he stands for.

A Brief History Of Rebellion

Reading the story of Noah reveals the genealogies of his sons: Shem, Ham and Japheth. Ham fathered Canaan who, in turn, had many sons, a number of whom are mentioned in Deuteronomy.

In Genesis chapter nine we read that Ham showed disrespect to Noah, incurring his wrath and prompting him to pronounce a devastating curse upon Ham's family: " 'Cursed be Canaan! The lowest of slaves will he be to his brothers.' He also said, 'Blessed be the Lord, the God of Shem! May Canaan be the slave of Shem' " (Genesis 9:25f).

What relevance does this curse have to Joshua? Leaving aside Japheth's lineage, Ham's descendants became the Canaanites, Egyptians and Philistines. Shem's descendants consisted of the Hebrews, Chaldeans, Assyrians, Persians and Syrians.

A clearer picture emerges when God led Abram, later named Abraham, a Chaldean, from Ur to Canaan. Isaac, Jacob and the entire Jewish nation were his descendants so, when Joshua and the Hebrews entered the Promised Land, they merely fulfilled the curse declared by Noah hundreds of years earlier, "May Canaan be the slave of Shem" (Genesis 9:26).

Is it any wonder that Rahab said to the spies who entered Jericho, "I know that the Lord has given this land to you and that a great fear of you has fallen on us, so that all who live in this country are melting in fear because of you" (Joshua 2:9)? Apart from hearing about the recent Hebrew victories, the Canaanites knew that history was against them.

Canaan became a nation of city-states. Listed in Deuteronomy chapter seven, their names expressed their characteristics. One of the largest and strongest nations in the area, the Hittites ("sons of terror") provoked fear in all who encountered them. The name "Amorite" means "the high one". They were tall, warlike people who lived in the mountains and were at one time considered to be the most powerful pagan nation in the area. Moses described Og, an Amorite king, as "the remnant of the Rephaites. His bed was made of iron and was more than thirteen feet long and six feet wide" (Deuteronomy 3:11). A giant indeed!

The names "Hivite" and "Perizzite" denote a villager or someone who has a poor view of their character and life, and it appears that they also had little regard for others. Genesis chapter 34 recounts the story of Shechem the Hivite acting inappropriately to, possibly even raping, Dinah, Jacob's daughter. In reading the chapter, we can see the consequence of such behaviour increasing the separation between the children of promise and those living under the curse.

Finally, the meaning of the name "Jebusite" is to "trample down". Jebus is believed to be the original Jerusalem, the centre of Jewish worship and rule. Joshua was unable to conquer the Jebusites fully, and they continued to be a thorn in Israel's side for many years after the conquest.

These enemies were not going to be miraculously removed from the land; Joshua had to engage in physical combat. God told him to destroy everything about these people or they would defile the "set-apart" nation.

What was so bad about the Canaanites?

Canaanite Religions

Ham, Noah's son, had experienced an amazing miracle. He was one of the chosen few to survive the devastation of the earth during the flood, and he knew first-hand of God's power and of his mercy. But despite this first-hand experience, Ham, his son Canaan, and their descendants rebelled against God. Over time, the Canaanites found religion. Unfortunately, it had nothing to do with their Creator. The supreme deity in the Canaanite religion was called El, a god whose main characteristic appeared to be uncontrolled lust. Not surprisingly, his worship involved orgiastic feasts, sacred prostitution, and child sacrifice (Deuteronomy 12:31). The gods Baal and Asherah, mentioned frequently in the Old Testament, were said to pursue a thoroughly physical relationship, despite being the son and daughter of El.

Anath, Astarte and Asherah were the Canaanite patronesses of sex and war, encouraging lust, bestiality, violence and murder, all of which figure strongly in their cultic worship. Serpent symbols were typical illustrations in their temples.

The cities of Sodom, Gomorrah, Ashdod and Gaza had temples dedicated to these gods; their object of worship and demonic expression of worship were the antithesis of all God stood for. Not surprisingly, God's call to Joshua was to destroy everything that had been contaminated by sin. Compromise would result in a watering-down of God's edicts, ultimately resulting in fleshly rather than Holy Spirit worship. God fully understood the nature of the human heart, and that if the nation of Israel failed to see him as the one true God, they would eventually blend in with every other polytheistic religion in the area. Moses had repeatedly warned the people of the need to stay away from the inhabitants of the land: "When you enter the land the Lord your God is giving you, do not learn to imitate the detestable ways of the nations there" (Deuteronomy 18:9). "Otherwise, they will teach you to follow all the detestable things they do in worshipping their gods, and you will sin against the Lord your God" (Deuteronomy 20:18).

A similar command is found in the New Testament: "Do not be yoked together with unbelievers. For what do righteousness and wickedness have in common? Or what fellowship can light have with darkness? What harmony is there between Christ and Belial? What agreement is there between the temple of God and idols?" (2 Corinthians 6:14–16a).

What About Us?

So much for history. What about our journey into the Promised Land? What will confront us as we seek rest in God? What are your Hittites, Girgashites, Amorites, Canaanites, Perizzites, Hivites and Jebusites? If we are to believe the definition of their names, what are you afraid of? What are the giants in your life? What trade-offs are you engaged in? Do you think little of yourself (*I'm not able to do this*), or of others (issues of leadership, authority, control)? Are you worshipping anything or anyone other than the Lord?

Just as the Israelites had to fight for their inheritance, each woman must overcome the barriers that prevent her from knowing experientially what it is to be seated in the heavenlies with Christ and blessed with *every spiritual blessing* (Ephesians 1:3). Addressing your giants, no matter how big, brings the freedom we seek in Christ. Take heart: "No man [or woman] will be able to stand against you. The Lord your God, as he promised you, will put the terror and fear of you on the whole land, wherever you go" (Deuteronomy 11:25).

I encourage you to read the book of Deuteronomy and ask God to reveal his word to you for this particular period of your life.

Know Your Boundaries

"I will give you every place where you set your foot, as I promised Moses. Your territory will extend from the desert to Lebanon, and from the great river, the Euphrates – all the Hittite country – to the Great Sea on the west. No one will be able to stand up against you all the days of your life" (Joshua 1:3–5).

The Israelites were given very clear boundaries by God. This fertile land was protected on every side by a desert, mountain range, sea or great river. These boundaries were not only to deter enemy invasion but also to discourage the Israelites from going beyond God's remit.

> The land you are entering to take over is not like the land of Egypt, from which you have come, where you planted your seed and irrigated it by foot as in a vegetable garden. But the land you are crossing the Jordan to take possession of is a land of mountains and valleys that drinks rain from heaven. *It is a land the Lord your God cares for; the eyes of the Lord your God are continually on it from the beginning of the year to its end.* (Deuteronomy 11:10–12, emphasis mine).

Staying within the boundaries allocated by God guarantees his care and protection.

We may look at the boundaries God has given us and decide that they are too restrictive. The land over the mountain or beyond the great river may be far more to our liking and the temptation to explore those lands may be great. Indeed, there may be people we know and respect who live in those lands and seem perfectly able to worship the Lord and live a "full" life. Compared to the vast expanse of the known world at that time, God's gift of land to the Israelites may have *appeared* small, but it was enough to fulfil God's purposes and to bless them. As mentioned earlier, however small it may have seemed, the Israelites failed to take possession of all that they had been given.

Before we feel hard done by concerning the constraints God has placed on our lives, let us explore and possess all that is within our designated boundaries before we look elsewhere. After all, the grass may be greener on the other side of the fence, but it still needs mowing! *It is my belief that if we can possess all that God offers, we will not feel in need of more.*

Know Your Capabilities

Many women leaving a life of homosexual expression prematurely declare their freedom in Christ. It is true that they have left their "Egypt", and many have embraced their journey through the wilderness with a fortitude and commitment that are second to none. They have crossed the Jordan declaring "self" dead to the past and are determined to spread the good news and claim the world for Jesus. All of this is highly commendable.

However, the battle is waged on two fronts. True, there is an external conquest to be won, but that only occurs as victory is seized on the internal front. The enemies the Israelites faced challenged their commitment to God in areas such as trust, dependence and communication. As we face and resolve or overcome personal enemies and strongholds, our Christian character will be developed and matured, thus enabling us to know, express and live God's purposes in this life. The development and maturing of our "being" will equip us in the "doing" that is to come.

Our ultimate call is to rule with Jesus. Refusing to be conformed to the way of the world and seeking transformation through continual submission to Jesus will further equip us to know God's will for our earthly life and to fulfil this eternal role. All of this takes time, and there is always the danger that if we engage in the external conquest too soon, we will get hurt.

I know too many women and men who are either wandering aimlessly back into the wilderness, unsure of their future, or have returned to Egypt thoroughly disillusioned with the Christian life because of the injuries they have sustained in ministry. No soldier is ever thrown onto the front line after completing a mere twelve-week boot camp, and no woman, irrespective of her testimony and enthusiasm, should commit to such an undertaking.

"When Pharaoh let the people go, God did not lead them on the road through the Philistine country, though that was shorter. For God said, 'If they face war, they might change their minds and return to Egypt.' So God led the people around by the desert road towards the Red Sea. *The Israelites went up out of Egypt armed for battle*" (Exodus 13:17f, emphasis mine). It is interesting that the Israelites were armed for battle when they left Egypt, but God did not deem them *ready* for battle. Placing a spear in someone's hand does not immediately transform her from slave to warrior.

Good Preparation – The Key To Success

My father took great pride in his painting and decorating skills. Desperate to see the end product, I found Dad's laborious preparation a source of frustration, as I didn't care about sugar soap, masking tape, or sanding down the paintwork. Who cared about the various brush sizes, the "cutting in" or the cleaning-up process? I just wanted the room to be finished! Why wouldn't he just let me get on and do it?

Years and many walls and ceilings later, of course, my decorating skills emulate those of my dad. I soon learned the benefit of lengthy preparation. Not only is the application of paint much easier, but the quality of work created is far superior to a rush job. Now I can't imagine decorating a room any differently or ever settling for an inferior standard. I am my father's daughter.

Good preparation is also the key to a successful Christian

walk. Chapters one and two of Galatians give the reader some insight into the lengthy training (several years) Paul underwent before fully launching into his ministry among the Gentiles. And this instruction was in addition to the scriptural study he had received under Gamaliel! The apostles spent every day with Jesus for almost three years before he entrusted them to go on a small missionary trip without him (Luke 10:1–16). Why should our Christian walk be any different?

If we want to rout the enemy, eat of the fruit, drink of the milk and dwell in the Promised Land, we must prepare well. Build a secure relationship with God based on his word, learn the boundaries he has granted you, know your strengths and weaknesses and learn from other pilgrims. Let the Holy Spirit define and refine your walk. As we mature in God we will hear his voice with greater clarity.

> The Lord said, "My sheep hear My voice" (John 10:27), not My lambs. Young lambs do not follow the shepherd as much as they follow other sheep. Young Christians need to follow other Christians until they mature enough to know God's voice. In this sense it is wise to stay close to those who know Him better, but we can never settle for that as our ultimate goal – we must know the Lord for ourselves.[17]

It is pertinent now to consider some of the enemies we may encounter in the Promised Land. On reading the book of Joshua, it is clear that there is no one formula that can be applied to every encounter. Success for the Israelites was dependent on staying close to the Ark of the Covenant and being obedient to God's command. We would be wise to fol-

---

17. Rick Joyner, *A Prophetic Vision For the 21st Century* (Thomas Nelson, USA, 1999), page 93.

low suit. "When you see the ark of the covenant of the Lord your God, and the priests, who are Levites, carrying it, you are to move out from your positions and follow it. Then you will know the way to go, since you have never been this way before" (Joshua 3:3-4a).

Chapter Eight

Everyone Has A Jericho

"It is a blessed thing when we love what God loves, when we seek what God seeks, when we are in sympathy with divine aims, and are obedient to divine commands: for with such persons will the Lord dwell."

Charles Haddon Spurgeon (1834–1892)

Not A Small Problem

Faith in action opens the door to greater intimacy with God. The destruction of Jericho had nothing to do with military strategy and everything to do with listening to and obeying God's word. And what a bizarre word it was!

> March around the city once with all the armed men. Do this for six days. Make seven priests carry trumpets of rams' horns in front of the ark. On the seventh day, march around the city seven times, with the priests blowing the trumpets. When you hear them sound a long blast on the trumpets, make all the people give a loud shout: then the wall of the city will collapse and the people will go up, every man straight in. (Joshua 6:3–5)

With such a battle plan at least one could guarantee that the enemy would be surprised by the attack! When God says that his ways are not our ways (Isaiah 55:8f), he certainly isn't kidding!

Situated five miles west of the River Jordan, a key city in Palestine, and sporting fortified walls 25 feet high and sometimes up to 20 feet wide, the city of Jericho was no pushover. This was the first major obstacle to the advancing people.

Confidence In God

We can cross the River Jordan only when we have come to the end of self-effort; when we are tired of walking round in circles in the wilderness and are prepared to relinquish our ways and be ready *fully* to embrace God's agenda and method. The Israelites had done all that was required of them. They had crossed the Jordan, yielded their flesh to mass circumcision, renewed their covenant with God and celebrated the Passover.

Immediately after the Passover, the Israelites, who, except for Caleb and Joshua, had only ever eaten manna and quail, got to taste the produce of the land. Obedience brought them immediate blessing. Can you imagine the excitement? Manna and the occasional quail had been their only source of nourishment for 40 years! Provided by God, it was certainly adequate sustenance, but paled into insignificance compared to the riches now on offer. "The manna stopped the day after they ate this food from the land; there was no longer any manna for the Israelites, but that year they ate of the produce of Canaan" (Joshua 5:12).

A child expects the mother to provide food (sometimes miraculously!) whenever he or she is hungry. But maturity brings responsibility and adults have to provide for themselves, from the planning and purchasing to the partaking of the meal: hence, for the Israelites, the cessation of the manna and quail. If God had continued to provide, they would never have ventured any further than the west bank of the River Jordan. Fear of starvation stimulates action. However, it was for God to choose the target, impart the plan of action, provide the necessary power, and determine the time of attack. The Israelites' responsibility was to be ready and willing to obey.

The Captain Of The Host

"Now when Joshua was near Jericho... " (Joshua 5:13).

Conflict is imminent. Joshua is close to encountering his first major obstacle, and at the last minute the "commander of the army" makes an appearance. How often has God worked in your life at the eleventh hour? For me, he appears to do this with alarming regularity. Only by faith can I believe that his timing is perfect. My flesh has already devised plans B and C in case God makes a "no show"! His appearance signals the presence of God and the long-awaited word of encouragement for Joshua: "See, I have delivered Jericho into your hands, along with its king and its fighting men" (Joshua 6:2). With such assurance, Joshua is now ready to obey God's plan, however strange it may appear to the onlooker.

Weapons Of Mass Destruction

The Ark of the Covenant, seven trumpets and the voices of 40,000 men hardly constitute weapons of mass destruction. However, this was God's considered plan and he expected it to be followed in every detail. From the outset, God wanted all the inhabitants, Israelites and Canaanites alike, to know that he was the one true God who has the power to build up and the power to tear down. His sovereignty was illustrated in his use of tactics. Victory would not be found in human strength but in God's presence, God's methodology and in the obedience of his people. Many years later, the boy David demonstrated God's point when he faced Goliath, the Philistine:

"Today I will give the carcasses of the Philistine army to the birds of the air and the beasts of the earth, and the whole world will know that there is a God in Israel. *All those gathered here will know that it is not by sword or spear that the Lord saves; for the battle is the Lord's, and he will give all of you into our hands*" (1 Samuel 17:46b–47, emphasis mine).

Rosh Hashanah

To a Gentile like myself, the use of the trumpet, or shofar as it is known, meant very little until I did some research on the ram's horn. It was blown on the Sabbath, announced the New Moon, and was eventually used to proclaim the crowning of a new king. Even today the shofar is blown when a new Israeli president is sworn into office. But the most important use of the shofar is during the Jewish festival of Rosh Hashanah, or Feast of Trumpets.

"The Lord said to Moses, 'Say to the Israelites: On the first day of the seventh month you are to have a day of rest, a sacred assembly commemorated with trumpet blasts. Do no regular work, but present an offering made to the Lord by fire'" (Leviticus 23:23–25). Traditionally, this festival celebrates God taking stock of all his creation, including human beings; the judgment he makes on this day, Rosh Hashanah, determines the direction God takes during the coming year. The long blast sounded at the foot of the city's walls on that fateful day at Jericho certainly declared God's intention: to destroy the wicked and to bless his chosen people.

Seven noisy circuits of the city must have built up the Israelite expectations that God was about to declare his judgment on Jericho. The final long blast from the shofars heralded an almighty roar from the people: God's time was *now*!

"When you hear them sound a long blast on the trumpets, make all the people give a loud shout: then the wall of the city will collapse and the people will go up, every man straight in" (Joshua 6:5).

All of the city wall collapsed as one and exposed the frightened inhabitants. Considered impenetrable, the ramparts crumpled before God and his faithful people. The once invincible city and the all-powerful citizens became as nothing before the awesome God, and everything, except for Rahab and her family, was put to *herem*.[18] Joshua completed the rout by declaring a curse on anyone who attempted to rebuild the city (Joshua 6:26).

My friends, what Jericho are you facing today? Are the walls too high to scale, too thick to chip away at, and the circumference seemingly too vast to encircle? What weapons are you using to bring down this stronghold? Have you used up all of your own resources and willpower, and is your hope of ever progressing further into the Land fading each day?

The resources that were available to Joshua and his people are available to us today.

Resources

The Bible

"Do not let this Book of the Law depart from your mouth; meditate on it day and night, so that you may be careful to do everything written in it. Then you will be prosperous and successful" (Joshua 1:8).

The best weapon we have is the word of God, the Bible. As we ingest all that it says about God, self and the world in which we live, we will get to know the character of God. Sadly,

---

18. *Herem:* a dedication of all things to the Lord by means of their total destruction.

the Christian church remains largely ignorant of this easily accessible resource, and it is amazing that people place their full trust in Someone they barely know. The same people are careful where they invest their money, but remain largely ignorant of the Person in whom they have invested their soul! The strongest weapon we have to offset temptation, rebuke attack, and remain steadfast in our covenant with him is to know God's all-encompassing love for us as his children. I learn of his absolute commitment to me largely through reading the Bible, and I am secure in his promises because I know that they are all "yes" in Christ (2 Corinthians 1:20).

Hearing God's voice

"As I was with Moses, so I will be with you: I will never leave you nor forsake you. Be strong and courageous, because *you will lead* the people to inherit the Land I swore to their fore-fathers to give them" (Joshua 1:5b, 6, emphasis mine).

Moses had just died, and Joshua was to the east of the River Jordan with up to two million people in tow. As Moses' assistant for the past 40 years, Joshua knew exactly how obtuse and rebellious these people were. He had also been in the Promised Land before, and despite the obvious blessings, Joshua also knew that there was a pile of trouble waiting for him! "Now faith is being sure of what we hope for and certain of what we do not see" (Hebrews 11:1). Born into slavery in a foreign land, a trustworthy migrant for 40 years, and now the leader of a nation, Joshua had learned the importance of faith over the years. Even so, God still felt it necessary to encourage him.

Are you in need of a faith boost? Are you weary from your travels? Can you see no respite ahead? Not only do we need to read God's word, we need to hear his encouraging voice in our ear. The more we can distinguish his voice from the melée of other voices, the more our faith in him will grow. Faith builds up faith. Walk in the faith you have and ask him to gift you with more.

Jesus as our leader

"Then they answered Joshua, 'Whatever you have commanded us we will do, and wherever you send us we will go' " (Joshua 1:16).

Our Joshua is Jesus Christ himself. As we know him through the written word, and hear him through the power of his Holy Spirit living in us, we can confidently pledge our allegiance to him, knowing that all his ways are perfect and trustworthy (2 Samuel 22:31).

The above declaration came from the Reubenites, the Gadites and the half-tribe of Manasseh who had already agreed with Moses that their land would be on the east side of the Jordan. The agreement was conditional on them helping the other tribes conquer the Promised Land before returning east to their families and herds. The land took around seven years to conquer and it would be reasonable to assume that a number of those men died during that time, either through war or from natural causes, and never fully realised their plans. But they died in the service of Joshua and God. I don't know what your hopes and plans are, but are you prepared to lay them down in the interest of others and at the command of Jesus?

Freedom to obey

"And he ordered the people, 'Advance! March around the city, with the armed guard going ahead of the ark of the Lord' " (Joshua 6:7). "But Joshua had commanded the people, 'Do not give a war cry, do not raise your voices, do not say a word *until the day* I tell you to shout. Then shout!' " (Joshua 6:10, emphasis mine).

Because the reader knows the end of the story, it is easy to overlook the difficulty some of the Israelites must have had with this military strategy. In Old Testament times a personal relationship with God was restricted to a chosen few; therefore the two million ordinary people were not privy to God's plan and had to rely on Joshua hearing from him correctly. Approximately 40,000 of them, the armed forces, had to obey Joshua's command without question. Imagine the muttering that must have been going on in the ranks by the fifth day as they marched, seemingly without purpose, around the city walls! Proverbs 3:5f comes to mind: "Trust in the Lord with all your heart and lean not on your own understanding; in all your ways acknowledge him, and he will make your paths straight" (Proverbs 3:5).

I don't know what stronghold or besetting sin you may struggle with. I don't know for how long you have been faithfully walking around it, having Jesus central to your life and listening out for his next command. I don't know how many circuits you will have to walk. All I know is that I am sure the Israelites were grateful they didn't rebel against Joshua on the sixth day and miss God's blessing.

To not understand God's ways and yet still remain faithful and obedient takes a great amount of courage. There may be people, possibly even Christian people, decrying your effort as a waste of time and energy. If that is the case, may I encourage you to reread Hebrews chapter eleven and place yourself with the thousands, if not millions, who have gone before you, choosing obedience to God rather than leaning on their own interpretation of circumstances?

Maintaining A Perspective

It is hard to keep the bigger picture in view if our noses are squashed against the stronghold walls! The writer of Ecclesiastes despaired all the time he viewed everything from "under the sun", from a worldly perspective. It was only as he began to assess life from an eternal perspective, from "under heaven", that he could begin to see beyond his sense of futility. "There is a time for everything, and a season for every activity under heaven: a time to be born and a time to die, a time to plant and a time to uproot, a time to kill and a time to heal, a time to tear down and a time to build, a time to weep and a time to laugh, a time to mourn and a time to dance..." (Ecclesiastes 3:1–4).

Viewing life from an "under heaven" standpoint enables us to trust when we don't understand, press on when we would rather hibernate, and rejoice when it would be easier to despair.

Learning The Art Of Contentment

Few are content in this world. Amassing interesting friends, objects and a sound financial base appears not to satisfy even the most blessed of people fully. Contentment is a learned state that requires some degree of effort. St Augustine's well-known statement, "My heart is restless until it finds rest in thee," seems even more applicable now, centuries after it was written. We may have a number of reasons for being discontented, ranging from a state of being single and/or childless, or feeling generally misunderstood, to being repeatedly overlooked for leadership positions within the church despite our abilities and gifts. Discontentment may open the door to bitterness and the ultimate rejection of God. Romans chapter one spells out the downward spiral: "For although they knew God, they neither glorified him as God nor gave thanks to him, but their thinking became futile and their foolish hearts were darkened" (Romans 1:21).

Paul, the writer of Romans, also wrote, "I am not saying this because I am in need, for I have learned to be content whatever the circumstances. I know what it is to be in need, and I know what it is to have plenty. I have learned the secret of being content in any and every situation, whether well fed or hungry, whether living in plenty or in want" (Philippians 4:11–12). "But godliness with contentment is great gain. For we brought nothing into the world, and we can take nothing out of it" (1 Timothy 6:6f).

Accepting our single or childless state does not mean that we live a pain-free existence. Our wants may be to marry and/or have children, and it may take a great deal of time to work through our feelings of loss, disappointment, anger and the sense of unfairness regarding our circumstances. But to work through these feelings and ride the emotional flux means that we are learning the state of contentment. Sharp pangs of loss may still catch us unawares, but acknowledgment without despair is a sign that we are achieving that near-illusive state the apostle Paul is keen for us to possess.

The Joy Of God's Presence

There are many battles to face in the Promised Land, but to be seated in the heavenlies with Christ, not only in a legal but also in an experiential sense, enables each to gain an eternal perspective on life and equips every woman to experience godliness and contentment. To feel surrounded on all sides by our Father is to live in complete freedom and security.

You hem me in – behind and before; you have laid your hand
    upon me.
Such knowledge is too wonderful for me, too lofty for me to
    attain.
Where can I go from your Spirit?
Where can I flee from your presence?
If I go up to the heavens, you are there;
if I make my bed in the depths, you are there.
If I rise on the wings of the dawn, if I settle on the far side of
    the sea,
even there your hand will guide me, your right hand will hold
    me fast.
If I say, "Surely the darkness will hide me and the light
    become night around me,"
even the darkness will not be dark to you;
the night will shine like the day,
for darkness is as light to you.   (Psalm 139:5–12)

The joy of God's presence rarely has much to do with feeling happy, but everything to do with receiving the strength to continue.

God is either bigger than this darkness, or he is not God... I was standing by the side of a metal-framed bed in a four-foot by seven-foot cubicle segregated from other patients by threadbare, ill-matching curtains. It was near midnight in February 1995, and I had been admitted to the acute ward of the local psychiatric hospital. Perched on the cliffs overlooking the English Channel, I had only ever seen the imposing Victorian building from the beach below. I was about to be acquainted with the full experience.

Further detail is unnecessary, but as I got into bed that night, accosted by strange noises and activity, and unsure of the following day, let alone my future, I felt incredibly alone: *There has got to be more than this.*

The heat of the ward and the smell of stale cigarettes were oppressive, but as I lay down I noticed that my head was near the window. Through the fixed two-inch opening I could feel the gentle sea breeze on my face. I could smell the fresh salt air and I could hear the pulsating drag of the sea on the shingled beach below. All other noises faded as God gave me the gift of his presence through his creation. He offered me the peace that does, indeed, defy all understanding. My mind was far too muddled to hear and understand his voice, but he enabled me to know him through the senses of touch, smell and hearing. Comforted by his presence, I slept properly for the first time in months.

As difficult as it may seem to stay in the Land, face a particular enemy, and claim our inheritance, the richness of relationship with God is worth it.

> God Himself has given us as a gift of love to His Son. It is the work of God to cleanse us; our work is to yield to His cleansing and to keep faith in His ability. Be reassured: you have been captured by His love. Because of His love, you can become more honest about your weaknesses, face your fears, and bring your sins to the throne of God's great grace. Instead of rebuke, you shall find the hand of God's forgiveness extended towards you.[19]

Psalm 23

A mature faith is required to dwell in the Promised Land. Spurgeon suggests that a test of maturity is whether, even when facing mounting problems, we can declare the 23rd Psalm with increased confidence: "Even though I walk through the valley of the shadow of death, I will fear no evil,

---

19. Francis Frangipane, *In the Presence of God* (New Wine Press, Bognor Regis, 1994), page 40.

for you are with me; your rod and your staff, they comfort me" (Psalm 23:4). The "valley of the shadow of death" can mean different things at different times of our life. The valley may be some addiction we are addressing, or a wayward relationship that requires attention. Whatever the valley, the important thing to remember is that all valleys are temporary and are to be walked through. They are not dead ends, bereft of hope. Certainly the path may be narrow and the walls either side tall and imposing at times, but if we fix our eyes not on the size of the walls but on the path ahead, and on Jesus our Good Shepherd, we will continue to deepen our relationship with God with every step.

> In his great mercy he has given us new birth into a living hope through the resurrection of Jesus Christ from the dead, and into an inheritance that can never perish, spoil or fade – kept in heaven for you, who through faith are *shielded by God's power* until the coming of salvation that is ready to be revealed in the last time. In this you greatly rejoice, though now for a little while you may have had to suffer grief in all kinds of trials. These have come so that your faith – of greater worth than gold, which perishes even though refined by fire – may be proved genuine and may result in praise, glory and honour when Jesus Christ is revealed. (1 Peter 1:3–7, emphasis mine)

God promises never to leave or forsake us, and that includes those dark valley moments when we feel all alone. I once heard a pastor say that a Christian life is not singled out because of its absence of shadow, but because of the presence of Jesus.

Perseverance

Be encouraged. As we persevere we will become more like Jesus. As we allow the Holy Spirit to transform us in mind, body and spirit, we will become more like him. Whether you are facing your Jericho or one of the other strongholds or enemies in the Land, take heart. Whatever your greatest struggle is today, it doesn't mean that it will be of equal power in six months' time. You never know, you may experience a "Jericho moment" and the problem may not even exist by this time next year! We can't gauge how long any aspect of discipleship takes before we live it, but we will change and increasingly become partakers of our inheritance.

Chapter Nine

Deceived Or
Deceiver?

"Good and upright is the Lord; therefore he instructs sinners in his ways. He guides the humble in what is right and teaches them his way. All the ways of the Lord are loving and faithful for those who keep the demands of his covenant." (Psalm 25:8–10)

Joshua's Curriculum Vitae

At any given moment, every one of us is merely a breath away from either including or excluding the Lord in our decision-making.

Beginning life as a slave to the Egyptian pharaoh, Joshua had witnessed the mighty miracles God performed as he secured the Hebrew release from captivity. He had been a bystander as God unleashed ten plagues on the oppressors, parted the Red Sea, and brought forth drinking water from a rock. Unbelievably, eating manna dropped daily from heaven must have become part of Joshua's *normal* life over the 40-year journey in the wilderness. As they approached Canaan, he showed his fearless, faith-filled fighting against the Amalekites and was rewarded with an opportunity to draw even closer to God. Throughout the expedition Joshua continually proved himself to be one "set apart", and while other Hebrews worshipped at their own tent some distance away, Joshua would actually enter the Tent of the Meeting with Moses: "The Lord would speak to Moses face to face, as a man speaks with his friend. Then Moses would return to the camp, but his young assistant Joshua son of Nun did not leave the tent" (Exodus 33:11).

His faith was such that he was one of only two spies to return from Canaan with a favourable report. As we read through Exodus, Numbers and Deuteronomy we find that his mentor, Moses, had imparted something very significant to his young assistant. Moses did not limit his teaching to the works of God, magnificent as they were, but trained Joshua to foster intimacy with God. He had taught Joshua to walk humbly before the Lord, cultivating his spiritual life so that when God's call came to lead the nation into the Promised Land, Joshua would be spiritually mature to respond.

So, with such a track record, why did Joshua fail to bring God into his decision-making regarding the Gibeonites?

Need For A Break

Life in the Promised Land had not proved to be a walk in the park. A seemingly impenetrable stronghold, Jericho, had been destroyed, resulting in much celebration, but Joshua's presumption and Achan's sin resulted in subsequent defeat in the small city of Ai. This defeat rocked the people and gave hope to the kings west of the Jordan, who now realised that Israel was not the invincible people they had once feared.

Repentance followed defeat. Having dealt with Achan and his family, the Israelites adhered to God's plan, producing a resounding victory against Ai. An altar was built, sacrifices were made, and Joshua read from the Book of the Law. All appeared well. The Israelites had learned their lesson, were encamped with the Ark at Gilgal, and were restored in their relationship with God.

But there is always a consequence to our actions. Although the initial defeat against the lowly city of Ai had been rectified, this failure resulted in an amalgamation of various Canaanite kings intent on waging war against Israel. Claiming the land was about to get a lot harder. Joshua and his men were doubtless aware of the gathering masses and upcoming battles, so is it any wonder that a group of travellers offering peace was seen as a welcome relief from the impending trials?

Ensnared By A Gibeonite

Two elements of the same enemy are at work here. In the distance is the overt enemy, banding together ready to launch an attack, and in the foreground the covert element, arriving, as it were, under the radar. The phrase "Never judge a book by its cover" has rarely been so apt.

Unchallenged and unhindered, the Gibeonites entered God's camp and spoke directly to the leader. To the naked eye their claim appeared genuine: their clothes were worn, their bread mouldy, and their wineskins empty and cracked. "The men of Israel sampled their provisions but did not enquire of the Lord" (Joshua 9:14). Flattery and a submissive attitude undermined the leader's initial caution and a treaty was ratified by an oath. Independent thinking and lack of prayer reopened the door to sin. Joshua knew that he was to destroy and not accommodate the inhabitants of Canaan, yet his poor choice severely hindered future Israelite claims on the land. So often, the covert attack can prove to be the most deadly.

Have you been ensnared by "Gibeonites"? With the proliferation of religious radio and television channels, the availability of the Internet, and the numerous books published on a weekly basis, it is easy for the believer to be sidetracked by a silver tongue. The apostle Paul warns us to be on our guard: "For such men are false apostles, deceitful workmen, masquerading as apostles of Christ. And no wonder, for Satan himself masquerades as an angel of light. It is not surprising, then, if his servants masquerade as servants of righteousness. Their end will be what their actions deserve" (2 Corinthians 11:13–15).

Satan's language must be recognised. "When he lies, he speaks his native language, for he is a liar and the father of lies" (John 8:44).

Did God Say?

It is hard to ignore the current debate among Christians regarding the issue of homosexuality. The dispute regularly makes the front page of every newspaper from the lowest tabloid to the most respectable broadsheet. I hardly think this debate does much to further God's kingdom, and while whispers and counter-whispers are murmured in the corridors of Lambeth Palace, thousands of men and women die daily outside a relationship with Christ.

Leaving aside the ongoing discussions regarding translation and other worldwide discussions, challenges come daily from well-intentioned friends who only want you "to be happy". The sentences often begin:

"God wants you to be happy, so..."
"Surely a loving God..."
"But you need..."
"You have a right to..."
"It's not good for man to be alone, so..."

All of the above are sub-questions to the first question in the Bible, "Did God say...?" The serpent sidled up to Adam and Eve. There was nothing aggressive in his body language or manner, because Satan knew that all he had to do was plant a seed of doubt and let the natural self do the rest. "When the woman saw that the fruit of the tree was good for food and pleasing to the eye, and also desirable for gaining wisdom, she took some and ate it" (Genesis 3:6). Despite residing in Eden, in the presence of God, Eve was deceived by a friendly overture from Satan.

Centuries later, despite being a truly godly man, Joshua, too, was conned into stepping outside God's remit. Should we be surprised when modern-day Gibeonites encourage us to compromise our faith? After all, they say, we are not being asked to give up our Christianity, just to bring it into 21st-century living and merge with the society in which we live.

Beware The Voice Of Reason

One of the great weapons of Satan is that he offers the voice of reason. Once a seed of doubt has been planted in your mind, he waters it with reasonable solutions to your presenting problem. In 1 Samuel 13, Saul fails to wait for a priest to offer the sacrifices and takes matters into his own hands. When challenged by Samuel he replies, "When I saw that the men were scattering, and that you did not come at the set time, and that the Philistines were assembling at Michmash, I thought, 'Now the Philistines will come down against me at Gilgal, and I have not sought the Lord's favour.' So I felt *compelled* to offer the burnt offering" (1 Samuel 13:12, emphasis mine). Saul's reasoning cost him the kingdom.

King David slept with another man's wife and made her pregnant. To cover his sin, David recalled Uriah, the husband, from the front line of battle and tried to make him sleep with his wife, Bathsheba. For two nights, despite being made drunk by David, Uriah chose not to enjoy his wife's company in consideration of the other soldiers. Thwarted by Uriah's honourable stance, David adopted another tack: "In the morning David wrote a letter to Joab and sent it with Uriah. In it he wrote, 'Put Uriah in the front line where the fighting is fiercest. Then withdraw from him so that he will be struck down and die'" (2 Samuel 11:14f). David's reasoned solution incurs God's wrath and, despite David's repentance and God's forgiveness, the king was plagued with family rebellion and death from that day on.

Isaiah chapter 36 speaks of the siege of Jerusalem. Having conquered everyone in his way, the Assyrian field commander challenges the entrapped Israelites' faith that had been placed firstly in Egypt (verse 6) and then in God (verse 7): "Do not listen to Hezekiah. This is what the king of Assyria says: Make peace with me and come out to me. Then every one of you will eat from his own vine and fig-tree and drink water from his own cistern, until I come and take you to a land like your own – a land of corn and new wine, a land of bread and vineyards" (Isaiah 36:16f).

Reasonable Or Right?

So often, the voice of Satan offers the semblance of God without the power. Engaging in a monogamous gay Christian relationship is a compromise paying only lip service to God's ways. It is akin to taking up Assyria's offer and enjoying the corn, new wine, bread and vineyards that are "a land like your own" (Isaiah 36:17). Although it may be similar to the Promised Land, *it is not the land chosen by God*. It is being well and truly encamped in the land of Satan.

The benefits and feel-good factor can imply that one is in God's will, but it is a deception. Outward trappings do not necessarily prove you are right with God.

Similarly, staying in the city, feeling surrounded, trapped and starving, as the Israelites did, does not mean that you have fallen out of favour with God! Careful reading of Isaiah 10:24-27 indicates that the prophet had already declared the safety of Jerusalem. Assyria, despite all its threats, was not going to succeed. What was required of the inhabitants was to trust God and wait for his deliverance.

When presented with any solution, we must resist the temptation to make an immediate decision. The solution may be reasonable but wrong. Conversely, it may be reasonable and right. Similarly, the solution offered may seem bizarre and may require further consideration before it can be considered either right or wrong. Remember: the decision to walk around the city walls, resulting in the downfall of Jericho, was both bizarre and right!

Am I A Gibeonite?

The Israelites were commanded to embrace aliens who were willing to recognise the sovereignty of God and the Hebraic claim on the land: "Do not oppress an alien; you yourselves know how it feels to be aliens, because you were aliens in Egypt" (Exodus 23:9).

Rahab's story is a case in point. Although originally destined to be part of the complete destruction of Jericho, her faithful response and commitment to God ensured her survival in both the temporal and eternal sense. Records show how God blessed Rahab's confidence in him. The Gibeonites, too, knew the power of God but chose resistance rather than repentance, their intention being to blend in with the Israelites without ever committing to the cause. Submission and worship were not on the agenda; their sole aim was survival. The ruse saved their lives but did not bring freedom.

Even when the truth about their identity emerged, the Israelites were powerless to act, thanks to an oath undertaken by the leadership. However, Joshua delivered a curse on the Gibeonites: "You are now under a curse. You will never cease to serve as woodcutters and water-carriers for the house of my God" (Joshua 9:23). "And that is what they are to this day" (Joshua 9:27b). The Gibeonites remained under the care of the Israelites and, because of their jobs, they remained close to God's presence. However, as slaves they were unable to enjoy the liberty of worship and the adoption of sonship enjoyed by the Israelites and the repentant aliens.

"Those who cling to worthless idols [their own ways] forfeit the grace that could be theirs" (Jonah 2:8).

Are You A Gibeonite?

I don't know your motivation for reading this book, but it is possible that some of you are currently engaged in a physical homosexual relationship while attending church and worshipping the Lord. Do you feel as though you are living life in the outer courts rather than sitting in God's presence in the Holy of Holies? Do you feel like God's adopted daughter or a foster child, always aware that you may be moved on? Your eternal life is secure, but is it a life of freedom, or is it plagued with intermittent waves of insecurity or guilt or a feeling that you have somehow sold yourself short?

If you are in any doubt, if you feel as though you have listened to the voice of reason rather than the voice of God, then it is not too late to lay down the trappings of a slave and pick up the garment of a "beloved child". We come to a God of mercy who longs to scoop us up in his arms and whisper words of love, encouragement and direction.

Are You An Assyrian?

I feel compelled to ask this question. Are you guilty of offering God's precious children a false land in which to dwell? Do you see their need and tender a facsimile of God's provision, luring them away from his narrow path with the promise of their own vines, fig trees and cisterns? In offering a "land like your own", are you not only allowing homosexual behaviour within your fellowship, church or ministry, but actually encouraging these sinful actions? These are not my words, but the words of our Lord that I humbly ask you to consider: "But if anyone causes one of these little ones who believe in me to sin, it would be better for him to have a large millstone hung around his neck and be drowned in the depths of the sea" (Matthew 18:6).

The Church's Problem

Church leadership would certainly prefer not to "have the problem" in the fellowship, or if the problem exists they would rather "it" would go away with healing prayer! Seemingly unchanging long-term issues produce too many questions for most local churches about God's desire or ability to act in an individual's life. Let's face it: living in the black-and-white world of easy answers offers far more security to the believer than living a life shuffling through the murky grey.

Yet, aside from the essential truth of repentance, salvation and eternal security, the majority of Christians do live in the greyness of life, either through their own decision-making or through unchangeable circumstances over which they have no control.

Living with unanswered questions despite being a born-again Christian goes far beyond the issue of sexuality and touches on every aspect of life, from birth to death and all points in between. The Protestant Church has a lot to learn from our Catholic friends when it comes to finding God in the uncertain, and not demanding a cut-and-dried solution to every problem.

Different Attacks Require Different Strategies

Warfare does not adhere to a simple "1, 2, 3" strategy, and tactics used in jungle warfare will achieve little success in an urban environment. A good soldier assesses the situation and acts accordingly.

We have already noted that the Israelites were presented with three different types of opposition early on in their conquest of Canaan. Jericho, known for its impenetrability, needed conquering. The five kings, relying on their strength of numbers and superior weapons, were planning a full-frontal attack and needed facing, and the Gibeonites, as we have just mentioned, placed their confidence in the successful deception of the Israelites. Faced with such a variety of opponents, any preconceived ideas of how the enemy would respond to the Israelite invasion could be abandoned within days of crossing the River Jordan.

The same is true for us. Spiritual warfare is waged on many fronts and requires our full reliance on Jesus if we are to be successful. There is no set pattern for warfare. A lone sniper can just as easily kill a soldier patrolling in the street as a machine gun can in the middle of a full-scale battle. This uncertainty ensures dependence on the guiding of God's Holy Spirit rather than reliance on human strength and intelligence. We do not possess the power or the wisdom to outwit the schemes of the evil one. That is why all thoughts, plans and behaviours must be filtered through the Lord before any action is undertaken. "His malice may be concealed by deception, but his wickedness will be exposed in the assembly" (Proverbs 26:26).

Come Out Of The Shadows

In conclusion to this chapter, not everyone is called to write a book or stand on a platform and expose their lives before any who would care to hear, but we are all called to live a transparent life: "They overcame him by the blood of the Lamb and by the word of their testimony; *they did not love their lives so much as to shrink from death*" (Revelation 12:11, emphasis mine).

Christ laid down his reputation in order to become sin, thus freeing us from eternal death. As we seek to walk in his footsteps, can we, too, lay down our reputation before other people and live in the honesty of our true testimony?

Seeing the back of a tortuous problem is inspiring and we need to hear those victorious stories, but our testimony of standing firm despite ongoing struggle, in whatever area, speaks volumes to those who silently grapple with fears, temptations and doubt.

There are three main directions we can take. The route of the Gibeonite will, if we are truly born again, subject us to the ever-stirring voice of God's Holy Spirit nudging us to reconsider our current path.

The second option is to present an image within the fellowship either of not having an issue with homosexuality or of having been "healed" from the problem. Fearing rejection, it is easy to fall into either of these camps. While the fear of exposure is very real and understandable, this lack of transparency ensures slavery to mediocrity, and such an ambiguous existence condemns a woman to pedantic Christianity, thus promoting frustration in her life and Christian service.

The third option, and in my estimation the most fulfilling, is to present oneself as Rahab did, exposed yet submissive to God. As we will read in the next chapter, Rahab's transparency eventually enabled her to fulfil God's purpose for her life.

Being an overcomer, in my estimation, is not about removing a thorn or weakness in our life. I believe it has a much broader application; it means being aware of Satan's desire to cause us to stumble, and attentive to God's ways of dealing with him. Most importantly, being an overcomer is being able to go to bed at night knowing that *today* you have been a faithful pilgrim on your particular journey.

Chapter Ten

Three Women
And A Baby

"As important as human affirmation is, it is woefully inadequate without God's affirmation of us. It is the knowledge that we are loved, accepted and valued by God that gives us a sense of value and true self-worth. When we are secure and confident in God's love, we grow out of our fears. When we know we are pleasing him, criticism and offences from others won't affect us as easily."[20]

Totally predictable in his attitude and yet quite unpredictable in his behaviour: such is the paradox of God. Not many would choose a pagan woman of ill repute as their instrument when faced with the need to destroy a stronghold boasting walls measuring three feet thick. But such were the plans of God.

Careful reading of Joshua chapter two offers much to consider. It appears that Rahab was converted before the spies arrived on the scene, and their appearance merely offered an opportunity to put her faith into deeds, thus illustrating the Christian walk later expounded in the New Testament book of James.

Despite the fact that the Canaanite city of Jericho was bereft of the Scriptures, or prophets declaring God's word, or any semblance of worship towards their Creator, Rahab responded to that which she had heard: the reports of God's miracle in parting the Red Sea 40 years ago and his more

---

20. Mike Bickle, *Passion For Jesus* (Kingsway, Eastbourne, 1994), page 151.

recent overthrow of the Amorites east of the Jordan: "When we heard of it, our hearts sank and everyone's courage failed because of you, for the Lord your God is God in heaven above and on the earth below" (Joshua 2:11).

The whole of Jericho had heard of God's power and their reaction was one of terror. Rahab had heard the same reports and responded in fear and conviction. Such is the grace of God, that he had gifted her with salvation faith. Even though the reports of God were second-hand, Rahab was able to make a life-saving decision. Conversion fosters change. Repentance means a change of heart and mind towards God, resulting in a change of conduct, and a change of attitude towards God's people.

"But she had taken [the Israelite spies] up to the roof and hidden them under the stalks of flax *she had laid out* on the roof" (Joshua 2:6, emphasis mine). Prostitutes do not bother themselves with the production of flax. Therefore one can conclude that Rahab's earlier conversion had prompted a change of occupation and, evident in her collusion with the spies, a change of attitude towards God's people. Clearly, she had crossed over from the camp of the ungodly and entered the household of believers.

Rahab is not the only biblical woman to risk all for the sake of the kingdom. Years later Ruth, the Moabitess, relinquished all in response to God.

An Unlikely Beginning

As mentioned in an earlier chapter, "Know Your Enemy, Know Your Boundaries", Rahab's ancestry derived from Noah's son, Ham. The Canaanites had rejected God in favour of many gods, and their worship incorporated evil practices such as child sacrifice and temple prostitution. Ruth's ancestry was no more laudable. Moab was the son of an incestuous relationship between Abraham's nephew, Lot, and his eldest daughter. The Moabite tribe lived on the east of the River Jordan.

In Genesis chapter 13 we read of Abraham giving Lot the choice of where to settle with his flocks and herds:

> Lot looked up and saw that the whole plain of the Jordan was well watered, *like the garden of the Lord, like the land of Egypt,* towards Zoar. (This was before the Lord destroyed Sodom and Gomorrah.) So Lot chose for himself the whole plain of the Jordan and set out towards the east. The two men parted company: Abram lived in the land of Canaan, while Lot lived among the cities of the plain and pitched his tents near Sodom. Now the men of Sodom were wicked and were sinning greatly against the Lord. (Genesis 13:10–13, emphasis mine)

Lot's story is one of compromise; he was willing to sacrifice his faith in the pursuit of a comfortable life. He not only wanted heavenly blessings but also craved temporal riches. He paid heavily for such a choice. Not so Ruth.

Like Rahab, Ruth's decision to follow God involved a separation from her country, her people, and the only way of life she had known. It wasn't as though her mother-in-law was offering an "unmissable deal". After all, Naomi was a widow, penniless, homeless and without prospects. She was a realist who never hid the difficult parts of her relationship with God from Ruth, so no rosy picture was painted to entice her daughter-in-law away from Moab. There was no "Come to Bethlehem and all will be fine," but rather the cost of settling in Bethlehem was spelt out to all who would hear. Yet Naomi's decision to return to Bethlehem, to the Promised Land, prompted Ruth to make a history-changing decision. She said to her mother-in-law, "Don't urge me to leave you or turn back from you. Where you go I will go, and where you stay I will stay. Your people will be my people and your God my God. Where you die I will die, and there I will be buried. May the Lord deal with me, be it ever so severely, if anything but death separates you and me" (Ruth 1:16f).

The citizens of Jericho did not share Rahab's faith, but Ruth had to contend with unbelief closer to home. Orpah, her sister-in-law, showed initial interest in returning to Bethlehem, but once the cost of commitment was made clear, Orpah, like her predecessor, Lot, chose to settle for the temporal comfort of Moab rather than throw in her lot with God's people. How many Orpahs do you know?

Risk-taking Response

Ruth and Rahab responded to God through what they heard, and in Ruth's case by how she saw another believer live. One is reminded of Lydia in the book of Acts:

> One of those listening was a woman named Lydia, a dealer in purple cloth from the city of Thyatira, who was a worshipper of God. The Lord opened her heart to respond to Paul's message. When she and the members of her household were baptised, she invited us to her home. "If you consider me a believer in the Lord," she said, "come and stay at my house." And she persuaded us. (Acts 16:14f)

Identification with the people of God is paramount. Isolated Christianity will lead to ultimate failure, so our commitment to God must be worked out in the fellowship of the believers. Lydia, a Gentile, invited Jewish men into her house. Ruth, after declaring allegiance to Naomi's people, immersed herself in the culture of Bethlehem. Rahab left her city, her occupation and income, her friends and customs, and entered the nomadic lifestyle of foreigners. I can't imagine that any of the women felt particularly comfortable with their decision. For Rahab and Ruth, there were probably times when they wondered just what they had done, but God proved himself faithful with every step they took.

The Outworking Of Faith

In the stories of Rahab and Ruth, it is easy to jump forward from their salvation moment to the blessing of their subsequent marriage and the part they played in the genealogy of Christ. But that would do them and us a disservice. Consider Rahab:

> Joshua said to the two men who had spied out the land, "Go into the prostitute's house and bring her out and all who belong to her, in accordance with your oath to her." So the young men who had done the spying went in and brought out Rahab, her father and mother and brothers and all who belonged to her. They brought out her entire family and *put them in a place outside the camp of Israel*. (Joshua 6:22f, emphasis mine)

How's that for gratitude and acceptance? Rahab was tolerable as long as she proved useful to the cause, the destruction of Jericho. The Hebrews kept their commitment and saved her and her family from the ensuing destruction, but considered them unclean and assigned them a place well outside the main body of people.

Ruth had married into a wealthy family (Ruth 1:21) and only became poor as a result of widowhood. She may have expected her commitment to God and emigration to

Bethlehem to produce immediate blessing. Instead, Ruth found herself dependent on the Jewish equivalent of welfare, and was reduced to gleaning grain from the edges of the fields.

In both cases, commitment to God brought isolation and hardship. What can have been their thoughts as they contemplated the outworking of their commitment? Was this the abundant life later promised in the gospel of John (10:10)?

The Testing Of Faith

"Consider it pure joy, my [sisters], whenever you face trials of many kinds, because you know that the testing of your faith develops perseverance. Perseverance must finish its work so that you may be mature and complete, not lacking anything" (James 1:2–4).

I possess an almost masochistic love for the book of James! Every line is like a barb digging into the flesh, reminding me of my inadequacies before God and others. Much as I may desire to live like a Christian Mr Magoo, oblivious to the chaotic reality of life, I find that my faith is tested on a daily basis. Sometimes the tests are basic and simply involve making a "yes/no" decision. Other trials can be difficult but short-lived, and there are those tests to my faith that are low-key in intensity but long-term in duration. I can shirk them, of course, but in so doing I forfeit the blessings that can be mine.

Rahab and Ruth faced immediate trials. Rahab, in her former life as a prostitute, must have known what it was to live on the margins of society. She had her uses of course, but for the most part was considered unclean and held in contempt. Unbelievably, the Hebrew response was no different from the Canaanite society she had left, so, not without good reason, Rahab could have become angry with God and bitter towards his people. She could have accused the Hebrews of hypocrisy and favouritism and would have had good grounds to gather her family and side with their fellow Canaanites in their opposition to the Hebrews.

We don't hear any more about Rahab until the New Testament, where we read that she married into the tribe of Judah, was the mother of Boaz and, according to the genealogy listed in Matthew chapter one, an ancestor of Jesus. She is cited in Hebrews chapter eleven as being a woman of faith and is commended by James for her deeds (James 2:25). Clearly, Rahab did not let her past, or her apparent rejection by the Hebrews, stand in the way of her relationship with God and the fulfilment of his purposes for her.

Ruth's life is more detailed. Although she faced an uncertain future in an unknown land, we read in Ruth 2:2 that her attitude was positive and practical as she humbled herself and procured work in nearby fields. Everyone noted her commitment to Naomi, and the owner, Boaz, singled her out for special attention. He offered her the full use of his fields and wells, companionship with the other women, and, noting Ruth's vulnerability, complete protection from the male workers. Boaz concluded by blessing her: "May the Lord repay you for what you have done. May you be richly rewarded by the Lord, the God of Israel, under whose wings you have come to take refuge" (Ruth 2:12).

Despite the hardship Ruth was encountering, she had come to trust God, shelter under his protection, and be confident of the truth later cited in Romans 8:28: "And we know that in all things God works for the good of those who love him, who have been called according to his purpose." And what a purpose! The apostle Paul wasn't exaggerating when he wrote to say that God can "do immeasurably more than all we ask or imagine" (Ephesians 3:20).

Although she would have been content to eke out a living gleaning from the fields, Boaz became Ruth's kinsman-redeemer and married her, thus securing her future comfort. Ruth had been married for ten years in Moab, but had not produced children. However, marriage to Boaz immediately produced a son, Obed, who was the grandfather of King David. Her faithfulness to God and commitment to his people had secured her place in the annals of Jewish history.

What About Me?

I can almost hear the murmuring from the reader: *It's fine for Rahab and Ruth; their faithfulness was rewarded with a husband, children and a "happy-ever-after" kind of life. That's not my story. Despite my faithfulness and commitment I'm still alone and I still feel isolated. What about me?*

Oh, for a straightforward answer! Perhaps if we were rewarded as a direct result of the effort and commitment applied over the years, our personal lives would be very different. It is easy to look around any congregation and conclude that recompense is granted to the seemingly undeserving and withheld from the diligent and godly! But such thinking would not promote godliness.

Consider Psalm 73. Asaph, a leader of one of David's levitical choirs, questions the justice of what he sees: the wicked are prospering while the godly struggle. For us, when the consequence of our decision to abandon homosexual behaviour in obedience to Christ does not, over time, result in a significant change of attraction, we, like Asaph, can be tempted to despair. *Why is my life so hard? Why can't I have a "normal" problem? Why doesn't God answer my prayers?*

Asaph bemoans the situation he sees until verse 17: "... till I entered the sanctuary of God... " It is in God's sanctuary that Asaph understands two things. The first is that comparing his fate with others separates him from God, and, secondly, he begins to appreciate the fundamental importance of his relationship with God:

> When my heart was grieved and my spirit embittered,
> I was senseless and ignorant; I was a brute beast before you.
> Yet I am always with you; you hold me by my right hand.
> You guide me with your counsel, and afterwards you will take
>   me into glory.
> Whom have I in heaven but you?
> And being with you, I desire nothing on earth.
> My flesh and my heart may fail,
> but God is the strength of my heart and my portion for ever.
> (Psalm 73:21–26)

When we are tempted to view our life as a half-empty glass of water, let us return to the fountain of life and recognise the steady stream of refreshing water that is available to all who care to drink.

Anna And The King

The story of Anna the prophetess is written in the space of three verses (Luke 2:36–38), yet speaks volumes to those who have "ears to hear".

Married in her mid-teens, Anna's life was mapped out before her: social and financial security, children and grandchildren, culminating in contented old age. But seven years into the marriage, and still without children, Anna's husband dies. No kinsman-redeemer materialises from the husband's family, and there appears to be no one from her line to assume her care. With no children to carry on the family name, Anna's future looks bleak. Although the translation is open to discussion, by the time she is mentioned in Luke, Anna has either been a widow for 84 years, or she is 84 years old and has been a widow for 70-odd years. Whatever the detail, we get the picture!

We know that the life of a Jewish widow was hard. In that culture, to be single and barren was shameful. How did she feel, living on charity? Did other women ridicule Anna and did passing men proposition her? We don't know. But what were her options? What was she to do now she lived on the periphery of Jewish society? "She never left the temple but worshipped night and day, fasting and praying" (Luke 2:37b). Anna threw herself on the mercy of God and chose to live in the temple courts. We don't know how she ate or where she lived or how she was clothed, but we can be confident that she was a living example of Matthew 6:33: "But seek first his kingdom and his righteousness, and all these things will be given to you as well."

Deepening her relationship with God became a lifelong passion, and she was released into a ministry of prophecy and prayer. Her devotion meant that she was at hand when Simeon prophesied over the eight-day-old Jesus (Luke 2:29–32). Simeon had had the luxury of being promised a sight of the Messiah before he died, thus enabling him to live with the expectancy of something great. Confidence in such a blessing gave him the freedom to leave the Temple and move out into the city, knowing that he wasn't going to miss anything of importance. Apparently, Anna received no such promise. She had nothing tangible to hold on to during her 84 years of devotion. And yet she remained faithful.

Jesus would not have been the only baby in the Temple

that day, as the law dictated that every first-born male had to be presented to the Lord. So one can only imagine the scene: the normal bustle of people going about their business within the Temple courts, plus anxious new parents, various wandering toddlers, noisy merchants and moneylenders, flocks of doves and pigeons for the numerous sacrifices, and finally all the bewildered, crying newborns!

In the middle of that melée, Anna set eyes on an eight-day-old baby boy and recognised him for who he was, the longed-for Messiah. Years later, even after witnessing miracles and listening to him preach, the disciples had trouble believing the claims of Jesus, and yet Anna was confident she had seen God's salvation. To recognise the fullness of God in bodily form was only a continuation of the relationship she had already developed with him over the years.

In the eyes of the world, Anna had lost much at a young age. Her future appeared austere and yet her vibrant faith and great expectations of God saw her through the lifelong difficulties, and in the midst of the continual struggles of life *she saw Jesus*.

Can you imagine this old woman weaving her way through the heaving masses, keeping her eyes fixed on this young couple and their baby? Can you imagine the ever-growing excitement she must have felt as she half-stumbled her way across Solomon's colonnade? She was about to hold in her arms the culmination of 300 prophecies uttered over thousands of years regarding the Messiah.

"The Son is the radiance of God's glory and the exact representation of his being" (Hebrews 1:3a). Here was the Saviour of the world, wrapped in swaddling clothes and placed in Anna's outstretched arms. "Coming up to them at that very moment, she gave thanks to God and spoke about the child to all who were looking forward to the redemption of Jerusalem" (Luke 2:38).

The Call Of Anna

It may be that our future position in society may resemble that of Anna rather than the married state of Rahab or Ruth. If that is the case, then let us, like Anna, use our singleness for the glory of God. I am sure there were times when she desired intimacy and companionship, a home and family, and a sense of feeling part of the "norm", but Anna persevered with God and, in the end, she saw her Saviour face to face. Her experience is our promise.

Chapter Eleven

Kinsey, Klein
And Schmidt

"We may not blame people for what they are, though we may for what they do. And in every discussion about homosexuality we must be rigorous in differentiating between this "being" and "doing", that is, between a person's identity and activity, sexual preference and sexual practice, constitution and conduct."[21]

Homosexual Hypotheses

Conspiracy theories abound about the deaths of Diana, Princess of Wales, J F Kennedy, and Elvis Presley. Was Diana's car crash really an accident or had someone close to her taken out a contract? What about JFK? Was his assassination the work of a single killer, the FBI, the CIA or the Mafia? And is Elvis actually dead? Or is he really working down at your local chip shop?

I am not, for an instant, claiming a conspiracy theory regarding the origins of homosexuality! However, there are plenty of theories around regarding the real reason why "we are the way we are". This book is not intended to explore and discuss the latest scientific findings or non-findings. Nor is it concerned with taking a particular stance just so that I can argue myself into an ever-decreasing spiral. I am no scientist or sociologist. However, we will look briefly at some of the current thoughts. It is my hope that you will glean what you

---

21. John Stott, *New Issues Facing Christians Today* (Marshall Pickering, London, 1999), page 384.

need and reject that which you find unhelpful as you continue your lifelong pilgrimage towards greater intimacy with God.

I am indebted to Thomas Schmidt, author of the book *Straight and Narrow? Compassion and Clarity in the Homosexuality Debate,*[22] for his clear presentation of various possible causations of the homosexual condition. Schmidt addresses six aspects of influence, offering the pros and cons for each area of study. The six aspects are as follows:

- biological
- cultural
- environmental
- moral
- behavioural
- volitional.

Biological
While a great deal of money has been spent researching a possible prenatal or early postnatal hormonal influence on an individual's sexual orientation, little can be concluded. Genetic research to date has failed to reach any definitive conclusion regarding a genetic base, and while I am very open to biological factors being part of the answer, it seems unlikely that biological findings *alone* will offer a completely clear understanding of homosexuality.

Cultural
Possibly because I have been able to trace a partial development of my own homosexual orientation through the theo-

---

22. Thomas E Schmidt, *Straight and Narrow? Compassion and Clarity in the Homosexuality Debate* (InterVarsity Press, Downers Grove, IL, 1995).

ries offered by the "social constructionists", I have welcomed their thoughts over the years. Social constructionism offers a four-stage overview of development: sensitisation, identity confusion, identity assumption and commitment.

The premise is that everyone is born with a heterosexual orientation (my jury is out on that one!), but some boys and girls become sensitised during pre-puberty through an awareness of feeling different from their same-sex peers and thereby don't seem to connect as a "real boy" or "real girl". Adolescence merely compounds those feelings, and that sense of being marginalised becomes associated with homosexuality. Years of confusion and feeble attempts to dismiss such thoughts may result, during late adolescence, in an acceptance of one's homosexual identity. This acceptance can offer, after long-term internal trauma, a real sense of belonging within the gay culture. For me, there was certainly an incredible awareness of "coming home" which contrasted dramatically with the years of feeling isolated and uncared for. Positive experiences ushered me into a commitment to my lesbian identity nurtured through friendships and long-term relationships.

However, like Schmidt, I don't believe social constructionism offers the complete answer. It implies that the individual is swept along on a tide of invariables, unable to influence a seemingly "etched in stone" predetermined path.

Environmental
Certainly, the high incidence of previous sexual abuse suffered by many women within lesbian society, most often from family members, requires much consideration. But sexual abuse is not the only reason to address environmental factors. "Interestingly, in the case of both male and female homosexuals, the loss of the father by death or divorce occurs

at an unusual rate. M T Saghur and E Robins, for example, found that 18 per cent of homosexual men and 35 per cent of homosexual women had lost their father by death or divorce before the age of ten."[23]

Through reading testimonies and talking to women over the years, I would also conclude that *emotionally absent* fathers, irrespective of their success in providing materially, also negatively influence a girl's development. In an attempt to emotionally engage the otherwise good father, a young girl may begin to over-associate with the masculine at the expense of the feminine. She will develop thoughts, behaviours and hobbies, vainly hoping to catch the beloved father's attention. Over the years this learned identification with the masculine becomes the only perspective the young woman has, and I have known this result in women not merely being attracted by a well-toned male body, but *wanting* that body shape herself!

An alternative scenario is that of a daughter who attaches more closely to an emotionally present father than to a perhaps less emotionally available mother.

Again, there are too many women who do not fit within these environmental profiles to endorse them solely as an accurate measure of the potential to develop lesbian attractions.

Moral

The moral climate in which we were raised strongly influences our thoughts, if not our behaviours. Having been nurtured in a family guided by strong, biblically-based values, many women are in conflict regarding their belief system and their lesbian feelings. No amount of bullying tactics from either the liberal

23. Ibid., page 144.

or the right-wing factions of Christianity will help a woman come to one of the most important decisions of her life.

Having made a decision to forsake any sexual expression of her lesbianism, it is most helpful for the individual to spend much of her time in company that will lovingly endorse that decision. Support and positive communal alternatives will help alleviate a potential social vacuum that could send a woman "back to Egypt".

Behavioural

In my totally non-professional opinion, I feel that behaviourists probably have more success in the study of animals than of humans! This theory is of limited applicability to homosexuality because it focuses more on a person's reaction to external stimuli than considering *why* someone behaves in a particular manner. And, like some of the other theories considered, the behaviourist theory appears to overlook the individual's potential input in determining her own life's path.

Volitional

Unless the woman is a victim of some kind of abuse, engaging in sexual activity involves choice. No matter how strong the desire, or available the opportunity, it is not *inevitable* that a woman engages in sexual behaviour. As difficult as it seems at times, "No temptation has seized you except what is common to [woman]. And God is faithful; he will not let you be tempted beyond what you can bear. But *when you are tempted*, he will also provide a way out so that you can stand up under it" (1 Corinthians 10:13, emphasis mine).

According to God's word, we will be tempted. Therefore, it is wise to have a plan of action already determined, long before the situation arises. Then, like any other crisis response plan, it will kick in as soon as the red button is pressed!

Thomas Schmidt: Multiple-Variant Model For Homosexual Identity Formation

Schmidt offers a model that I found helpful in sketching my own homosexual development: the emphasis is on the word "helpful". As Schmidt explains:

> The multiple-variant module itself is intended to aid conceptualisation, not to explain particular cases, because faulty memory and guesswork about variable strengths will always cloud the picture. Nevertheless, even an admittedly cloudy picture is better than no picture when we consider the powerful drive to understand and accept one's sexual identity – or to change it.[24]

I have replicated his model (see Figure 1 on the following page). If it helps in understanding Schmidt's chart, I will consider a fictional woman whom I shall call Rachel. (Again, please bear in mind that this is a simplistic overview.)

Rachel's mother experiences a non-traumatic pregnancy, and Rachel is born without any obvious genetic or hormonal problems (*biological*). She is the second child and first daughter of a white middle-class two-parent family. Although the family does not attend church on a regular basis, they uphold strong moral principles when it comes to issues such as honesty, hard work and community spirit. The children are well loved and cared for, and all is well within this perfectly normal "middle-England" family (*cultural, environmental, moral*).

At the age of six, tragedy befalls Rachel's family when her father is killed in a road accident while coming home from work (*environmental*). Family, friends and neighbours rally round, supporting them over the next few years. Eventually,

---

24. Ibid., page 153.

Figure 1: Multiple Variable Model for Homosexual Identity Formation[25]

normal *biological*

genetic or hormonal difference ▶ *cultural*

clear gender roles

societal or individual confusion ▶ *environmental*

functional family

family dysfunction ▶ *moral*

responsible

permissive or repressive ▶ *behavioral*

negative experience

positive experience ▶ *volitional* consent

refusal

25. Thomas E Schmidt, *Straight and Narrow?* (InterVarsity Press, Downers Grove, IL, 1995), page 152.

to Rachel's dismay, her mother meets, dates and eventually marries a man she met at work. The stepfather, Simon, is perfectly agreeable in all that he does, but Rachel, now thirteen, feels uneasy in his company (*environmental*). She cannot pinpoint any particular reason for this discomfort, but, no longer finding the house the safe haven it once was, Rachel chooses to spend more time around at friends' houses rather than confronting her increasing sense of disquiet.

Rachel's mother, Laura, senses an ever-increasing gap growing in the family unit, but seems powerless to change the scenario. Any attempts to discuss the situation result in Rachel's moody outbursts and a final slam of the front door. Family mealtimes, trips out, and general fun times no longer exist, and Rachel becomes increasingly influenced by her gang of friends as the base of influence shifts from the known to the unknown peer group (*environmental, moral, behavioural*).

Rachel, now 25 years old, admits that her life between the ages of 15 and 19 was rather lost. Failing most of her GCSE exams and not even attempting A levels placed her at a disadvantage when it came to career choices (*environmental*). Experimentation with drugs and regular bouts of binge drinking had done little to "fill the emotional hole". Alcohol-fuelled sex had left her feeling dirty and less than desirable, with a local reputation for being "easy". She had sought solace in a female friendship, which developed into a full-blown lesbian relationship (*environmental, moral, behavioural, volitional*).

Eventually, Rachel realises she is on a road to nowhere. Without funds or possessions, she returns to the family home (*environmental, moral, behavioural, volitional*).

Accepting responsibility for her behaviour, Rachel begins the restoration work with her mother and establishes an adult relationship with Simon, her stepfather. Over time

Rachel gains sufficient qualifications to attend college and pursue a career in design, and develops like-minded male and female friends (*behavioural, volitional*).

What I hope this chart and fictional case study indicate is that a multi-variant approach helps prevent the oversimplification of cause and effect in homosexual development and places responsibility for what one does in response to any possible causal factor back in the hands of the individual. It implies that there is no sense of inevitability about the development of an individual. We have all come across men and women who have appeared to have life stacked up against them, but who cite a relationship with a teacher or pastor who really helped turn their life around. Such is the flexibility of the model offered by Schmidt.

Kinsey And Klein

Merely refraining from sexual behaviour does not necessarily offer any insight into our inner motivations. However, closing the door to sexual expression enables us to look more clearly at the inner workings of our being.

Alfred Kinsey, a researcher working in the late 1940s, developed a scale explaining sexual behaviour as a continuum from exclusively heterosexual to exclusively homosexual. On this scale were numbers ranging from 0, declaring a person to be exclusively heterosexual, through to 6, labelling an individual as exclusively homosexual. Individuals placed their "x" where they felt it most appropriate. The rest of the numbers on the scale read as follows:

1   Predominantly heterosexual, only incidentally homosexual

2   Predominantly heterosexual, but more than incidentally homosexual
3   Equally heterosexual and homosexual
4   Predominantly homosexual, but more than incidentally heterosexual
5   Predominantly homosexual, only incidentally heterosexual.

There were many flaws in Kinsey's theory, particularly his sampling method, which might have skewed his results to portray the general population overall as being perhaps more sexually adventurous than was actually the case. In addition, other researchers sought to broaden the method of assessment so as to describe sexuality in more multidimensional terms.

The Klein Sexual Orientation Grid first saw the light of day in 1978 and was developed and refined before finally being published around 1985. It is far more complex than the basic Kinsey Scale, and includes the dimension of time more explicitly for sexual orientation, as well as sexual behaviour and identity. Questions are divided into three categories:

- the present (most recent twelve months)
- the past (up to twelve months ago)
- the ideal (what behaviour one hopes to engage in).

Questions regarding sexual orientation were also to be answered on three levels: the past, the present and the ideal. The list reads as follows:

Sexual Attraction: To whom are you sexually attracted?

Sexual Behaviour: With whom have you actually had sex?

Sexual Fantasies: Who are your sexual fantasies about? These fantasies or daydreams can occur at any time of the day.

Emotional Preference: Emotions influence, if not define, the actual physical act of love. Do you love and like only members of the same sex, only members of the other sex, or members of both sexes?

Social Preference: Social preference is closely allied with but often different from emotional preference. With members of which sex do you socialise?[26]

Lifestyle Preference: What is the sexual identity of the people with whom you socialise?

Sexual Identity: How do you think of yourself?

Political Identity: Some people describe their relationship to the rest of society differently from their personal sexual identity. For instance, a woman may have a *heterosexual* sexual identity, but a *lesbian* political identity. How do you think of yourself politically?

The aspect "political identity" was not on the original Klein Sexual Orientation Grid, but was added later by Keppel and

---

26. Please note that most single people predominately socialise with members of their own sex.

Hamilton[27] to encompass a broad range of thoughts, beliefs, feelings and influences.

Discernment Required

One can immediately see the benefit of broadening Kinsey's original scale. However, as a Christian who believes that all sexual behaviour should occur only within a heterosexual marriage, and that Christians should try to take every thought captive (2 Corinthians 10:5), I can't offer *carte blanche* approval of the Klein Sexual Orientation Grid.

Indeed, because of my behaviour (or lack of it), I can't actually answer all the questions, so am unable to arrive at any concrete conclusions! However, I do think it is most helpful in assisting an individual to explore where they have come from and how much change in their life has actually taken place. After all, the fruit of ongoing Christian maturity will bring about change of thinking and behaviour as we seek to live under the rule of Christ rather than pander to the call of the flesh. Self-assessment is necessary and can prove encouraging during those difficult pilgrimage times when, facing ongoing temptations, we may question that very maturing process.

Klein's research has shown that, for many people, some aspects of their lives have altered while other factors have remained the same. Therefore, my 19 years of celibacy (behaviour) have proved constant even though my emotional and physical attractions have experienced some fluctuation.

---

27. List adapted from an article written by Bobbi Keppel and Alan Hamilton, PO Box 10818, Portland, ME, 04104. (For your information: Bobbi Keppel and Alan Hamilton are co-founders of the Unitarian-Universalist Bisexual Network. You may or may not want to explore their work further.)

What Can Be Determined?

If any reader came to this book thinking that the origin of homosexuality lay in simple cause and effect, I hope this chapter has dispelled any such thoughts. Kinsey, Klein and Schmidt have shown that variations between individuals, despite perhaps a similar presentation of homosexuality, are as diverse as those between all people, irrespective of orientation.

Why do some people change in their attractions while others seem incapable of change despite high motivational factors and positive reinforcement? I really don't know, although I am inclined to be in agreement with Sonia Balcer, who states:

> The scientific evidence seems to suggest a complex interplay between genetic and environmental factors, with the implication that the operative components vary from individual to individual. That would mean that in those persons for whom the developmental factors are predominant, the effects of prayer and therapy could, as a matter of course, have a significant impact on the "direction" of attractions. However, for those persons in whom the inborn factors are predominant, the effects of prayer and therapy might be beneficial in many areas of life and relationship, but (apart from a distinctly miraculous shift) would be unlikely to bring about opposite-sex attractions.[28]

I would encourage further research along these lines of thought.

---

28. Author: Sonia Balcer. Sonia leads a ministry for people struggling with homosexuality and is one of the leading contributors to two websites encouraging dialogue between (or at least a Christ-like response towards) those who hold differing opinions regarding homosexual behaviour: www.bridges-across.org and www.justice-respect.org.

Chapter Twelve

Eunuch For Christ

"The true eunuch is not he who cannot, but he who will not indulge in fleshly pleasure."

Clement of Alexandria

"Most people simply lack the conviction to engage in such self-sacrifice."

Virginia Postrel, *Reason* magazine, October 1998

Sex In Society

Through choice I have never watched an episode of *Sex and the City, Will and Grace,* or *Couplings,* but I know enough from the promotional trailers to realise that none of them would be particularly helpful in my walk with God. I don't need a TV programme to fuel an already active imagination when it comes to serial relationships and sexual activity!

Western society, at least, appears to have reduced the vast concept of love down to the narrow field of mere sexual expression. Sniggering and innuendo have crushed subtle demonstrations of tenderness, affection, and filial love, especially among men, resulting in a reduction of platonic intimacy between people of both sexes. If you are not having sex three times a week, we are led to believe, then not only is there something missing in your life, but this sexual suppression may also endanger your long-term health.

Magazines, no longer limited to the top shelf, are crammed with articles on who is doing what with whom, and who should be doing something with someone else! Interspersed between the covers are other articles ranging from "How to Get Your Man" to "Ten Practical Steps to a Sparkling Sex Life" And what has this newfound freedom brought?

United Kingdom Statistics on Sexually Transmitted Diseases[29]

Since 1996, there has been a sustained increase in the diagnoses of most STDs in the UK. The following data is from a six-year study based on 1996–2002 statistics:

- Uncomplicated gonorrhoea has increased by 106%
- Genital chlamydia has increased by 139%
- Infectious syphilis has increased by 870%.

The total number of new cases of chlamydia in 2002 *alone* was 81,680. Of females with gonorrhoea and genital chlamydial infection in 2001, 42% and 36% respectively were *under 20 years of age*.

Society champions self-determination for the individual and applauds all forms of self-expression provided that "no one gets hurt". Yet the very freedom an individual craves is incarcerated in a plethora of addictions, broken relationships and stress-related illnesses. I am reminded of two scriptures that, although written thousands of years ago, could easily have been written last week: "There was no king in Israel at that time. Everyone did just as he pleased" (Judges 21:25, Good News Bible). "Where there is no revelation, the people cast off restraint" (Proverbs 29:18a).

A society without godly restraint abandons the individ-

---

29. Data taken from the Public Health Laboratory Service Report found on the following website: www.avert.org. [For some reason these statistics do not include Scotland.]

ual to his or her own sense of right and wrong based on that individual's current emotional state. How can such a fluctuating bottom line promote a sense of security and well-being?

Pressure From The Pulpit

Unfortunately, not all is well within Christendom. Historically, the church waxes and wanes between upholding firstly marriage and then singleness as the ideal state in which to live out the Christian faith. Recently, there has been some discussion over comments made by Dr Al Mohler, president of the Southern Baptist Theological Seminary, Louisville, Kentucky, USA at a large conference for singles. Part of the teaching was played over the airwaves and endorsed by the hosts of the programme, *FamilyLife Today*.[30] I tracked down the transcript of the programme and was stunned to find that the piece was entitled: "Fatherly Advice to Singles – Get Married".

I could partially understand the angle Dr Mohler was taking, and I am certainly not taking issue with all that he said. However, I do object to the following statement: "What is the ultimate priority God has called us to? In heaven, is the crucible of our saint-making going to have been through our jobs? I don't think so. The Scripture makes clear that it will be done largely through our marriages."[31] What Scripture is Dr Mohler reading? My understanding is that *God blesses both marriage and singleness*, and that *both* states require the fullness and empowering of God's Holy Spirit in order for an individual to become more Christlike in attitude and behaviour.

Neither marriage nor singleness is "the ideal" per se;

---

30. www.familylife.com.
31. Broadcast 22 June 2004.

surely, the ideal for an individual is fulfilling God's call on their particular life right now. Of course we can and do pray for situations to change and develop, but "we know that in *all* things God works for the good of those who love him, who have been called according to his purpose" (Romans 8:28). That "all" includes our jobs, hobbies, Christian service and, yes, our marital status.

I long for the church to cease promoting one state over the other and to explore ways in which both the married and the single, those with children and those without, can *together* stand apart from and influence the surrounding society.

Sounding A Contradictory Note

To be a disciple of Jesus Christ is to be a sign of contradiction: "Do not love the world or anything in the world. If anyone loves the world, the love of the Father is not in him. For everything in the world – the cravings of sinful man, the lust of his eyes and the boasting of what he has and does – comes not from the Father but from the world. The world and its desires pass away, but the man who does the will of God lives forever" (1 John 2:15–17).

It is my belief that sexual intercourse should be reserved for heterosexual marriage. As for me, despite the many changes in my life, I do not feel my sexual orientation has altered over the past 19 years to a point that warrants booking the church and ordering the wedding flowers! So, what are my options? If I am to remain true to what I believe the Bible is saying, then my only choice, *like any other unmarried Christian*, is to remain celibate.

It is not unusual for Christians, most of whom married around the age of 20 and now live comfortably with their children or in close proximity to their grandchildren, to remind me of the "gift" I have been given! Do I consider my 19 years of celibacy a gift from God? If they are, I have certainly received more welcome gifts in my lifetime!

I am sure some men and women see their celibacy as a gift from God, but I just don't happen to be in that particular group. I don't celebrate my celibacy as a gift but believe it is a choice I make in obedience to my Lord. Heterosexual sex outside marriage and homosexual sex between consenting adults are not illegal, so there would be nothing preventing me from engaging in such activity this very day. However, God's love constrains and his grace helps me remain faithful to his teaching.

Not only does God declare his will for us, in this case celibacy unless married, but he *enables* each to carry out his edicts not only through mere behavioural obedience (which was certainly true during the early years), but also because he actually changes our desire as the love relationship with him deepens and matures. "For it is God who works in you to will and to act according to his good purpose" (Philippians 2:13).

Mahatma Gandhi was right when he said, "Only a love that can match or exceed what is possible with sexual love can sustain celibacy." It is not enough merely to love God; we need to be "in love with God" and committed to him and his ways if we are to stand against society's daily emotional and sexual bombardment. A greater love has to exist between us if I am not to commit adultery, be it emotional or physical, against God. A number of years ago I bought a ring that I wear on the wedding finger of my right hand; it reminds me of my relationship with, and commitment to, my Saviour and Lord.

True Love

If I am to live out of a love that can not only match the intimacy of partnership and sexual love but exceed that love, then I had better know what kind of love I am searching for and need to express. I need look no further than the first letter to the Corinthians. "Love is patient, love is kind. It does not envy, it does not boast, it is not proud. It is not rude, it is not self-seeking, it is not easily angered, it keeps no record of wrongs. Love does not delight in evil but rejoices with the truth. It always protects, always trusts, always hopes, always perseveres. Love never fails" (1 Corinthians 13:4–8a). What a list! Have I upheld this expression of love in the past hour, never mind during the course of my lifetime? Despite its popular recitation at weddings throughout the land, surely no human love can attain such dizzy heights?

And yet God's love to us is all of those things.

God is so patient with me and perseveres in his commitment even when I waver in mine. The Bible says that he is "a compassionate and gracious God, slow to anger, abounding in love and faithfulness" (Psalm 86:15). As I confess my sins and recommit my ways to him, he promises to keep no record of my wrongdoing. God is truth and proves himself to be trustworthy and protective. Zephaniah 3:17 declares: "He will take great delight in you, he will quiet you with his love, he will rejoice over you with singing." How can I not respond to such an overture of love?

Open And Closed Doors

Quite frankly, it is far easier to jump into bed with your partner and pretend that 30 minutes of sexual "making up" solves all problems; it is far more challenging to explore ways of expressing affection, love and commitment to those outside the immediate sphere of partnership.

Submitting to God's call of celibacy is much more than not having sex. While closing the door to sexual expression, a celibate life demands that we open the door to a completely new lifestyle. It means we have to achieve a greater understanding of *agape* love: the unconditional love that God expresses towards each of us. For many, past relationships, even those basking under the banner of "long-term, loving, and committed", have been more about snatching whatever is on offer, hoping that our black hole of need can be filled and our tenuous sense of worth upheld by this imperfect love. Being single and celibate demands a deeper relationship with God if we are to experience contentment and fulfilment within this more restrictive framework.

Most importantly, celibacy, whether it is for a period prior to marriage or for a lifetime, should not be seen as a punishment or a second-rate condition, but as an opportunity to pursue intimacy with God at a depth rarely afforded to most Christians. We can have a waiting-room attitude that encourages a woman to "sit it out" until marriage comes along, or we can see singleness as a legitimate state in which to grow and thrive. This time, however short or long it may be, offers the opportunity to be responsible, dependable and trustworthy without expecting payback or living under the burdening questions: *Do they love me?* or *Will they leave me?* or *Will I ever live up to their expectations?*

As I read through that passage in Corinthians, it is clear that real love, *agape* love, is focused on the good of others and not merely on getting our own needs met. It is the antithesis to worldly living. To live under the teaching of 1 Corinthians 13, difficult as it is, is surely an opportunity to reflect Jesus.

The Ethiopian Eunuch

> So he [Philip] started out, and on his way he met an Ethiopian
> eunuch, an important official in charge of all the treasury of
> Candace, queen of the Ethiopians. This man had gone to
> Jerusalem to worship, and on his way home was sitting in his
> chariot reading the book of Isaiah the prophet... The eunuch
> was reading this passage of Scripture:
>
> "He was led like a sheep to the slaughter,
> and as a lamb before the shearer is silent,
> so he did not open his mouth.
> In his humiliation he was deprived of justice.
> Who can speak of his descendants?
> For his life was taken from the earth."
>
> (Acts 8:27, 28, 32, 33)

Have you ever read a scripture that pierces you right to the
core, a scripture that has your name "written all over it"?
Surely this was the case for the Ethiopian official.

Isaiah prophesised that the Messiah would be humiliated
before all, deprived of basic human rights and "cut off" without leaving a wife or children, a truly shameful position for a
man of that time. Indeed, part of the Talmud[32] states: "The
unmarried person lives without joy, without blessing and
without good... an unmarried man is not fully a man"
(Yevamot 62b–63a).

The Ethiopian, despite being in a position of privilege
and power and enjoying a comfortable lifestyle, had experienced the humiliation, not to mention pain, of castration. He
now lived with the reality of lifelong singleness and childlessness and certainly stood outside the realms of conven-

32. Talmud: oral law committed to writing by rabbis, initially around 220
AD.

tional blessing. The book of Acts tells us that the Ethiopian had travelled hundreds of miles to Jerusalem with one specific purpose in mind, to worship God.

It is not known whether he knew the law or not, but according to Deuteronomy 23:1, no eunuch was allowed to enter the Temple. So, even when he turned to God for blessing, the religious laws of the day denied the eunuch access.

What would your response be to such rejection? Surely you would feel alienated from both society and God, giving you sound foundations to dismiss everyone and everything and become bitter over such injustice. The eunuch, however, looked to the Scriptures, read of the coming Messiah and could empathise with him:

> In his humiliation he was deprived of justice.
> Who can speak of his descendants?
> For his life was taken from the earth.

With the help of the evangelist Philip, especially provided by God, the Ethiopian was able to understand more of this Messiah and commit to him. And can you imagine the amazement of the Ethiopian when he read further from the book of Isaiah?

> Let no foreigner who has bound himself to the Lord say, "The Lord will surely exclude me from his people." And let not any eunuch complain, "I am only a dry tree."
>
> For this is what the Lord says: "To the eunuchs who keep my Sabbaths, who choose what pleases me and hold fast to my covenant – to them I will give within my temple and its walls a memorial and a name better than sons and daughters; I will give them an everlasting name that will not be cut off. (Isaiah 56:3–5)

With such a promise to cling to, is it any wonder the eunuch "went on his way rejoicing" (Acts 8:39b)? That promise from Isaiah holds true for each of us today. Do you feel somewhat separated from the church norm of marriage and children? Have you been made to feel unwelcome in your church because of your homosexual struggles? Do the next 40 years or so of possible singleness cause bouts of helpless depression? Let us, like the Ethiopian, not turn from God, but turn to Jesus for encouragement: "For we do not have a high priest who is unable to sympathise with our weaknesses, but we have one who has been tempted in every way, just as we are – yet was without sin. Let us then approach the throne of grace with confidence, so that we may receive mercy and *find grace to help us in our time of need*" (Hebrews 4:15f, emphasis mine).

It takes little effort to absorb the faulty messages we are often sent from secular and church society alike, but, whatever we may have been dealt in life or whatever stressors we have to face, the truth is that we, as believers, have our names written in the "Lamb's book of life". I may not have physical children to continue my earthly line, but I have entered into eternal life through the reconciling work of Jesus Christ. And, Lord willing, in my service to him over the years, I also have spiritual children whom I will one day meet in heaven.

One Man's Legacy

The converted eunuch continued his journey back to Ethiopia. He had no believer in Jerusalem to check on his progress, and there are no indications that Philip did any post-conversion follow-up work. There was no loving fellowship in his home country to befriend or disciple him through the early years, and, owing to his condition, this man would never marry or father children. On the face of it, one would-n't really consider his life blessed.

Yet today, according to the 2003 Ethiopia Religious Freedom Report,[33] out of the population of 71 million, the Ethiopian Orthodox Church claims 31 million believers spread throughout 110,450 churches. Despite the large numbers of Muslims in the country, the report also says that Evangelical and Pentecostal Protestantism are the fastest-growing faiths, claiming 7.4 million members!

Although this treasury official had no blood family to remember him, his life and commitment is still remembered 2,000 years later, and his story will continue to be read and studied until Christ returns: rejected by his fellow human beings, rejected by formalised religion, but accepted and blessed by God.

Jesus Did Say...

"For some are eunuchs because they were born that way; others were made that way by men; and others have renounced marriage because of the kingdom of heaven. The one who can accept this should accept it" (Matthew 19:12).

Undoubtedly, there are a number of ways in which this verse can be interpreted. We have just considered the Ethiopian who was "made that way by men", and I am sure that practice still occurs in certain parts of the world. But I venture an interpretation that applies specifically within the confines of homosexuality. Some may accuse me of abject simplicity and theological ignorance, but, based on Jesus' statement above, I offer the following thought to ponder:

There are some women unable to enter into heterosexual

---

33. Report found on the following website: www.about.com.

relationships because their innate make-up prevents them from feeling attracted to men. Others have responded to their upbringing in such a way that they feel attracted only to members of their own gender. And there are those women who feel physical and emotional attraction towards men, but choose not to express, even within marriage, those attractions in order to fulfil the purpose to which God has called them.

Jesus' final sentence, "The one who can accept this should accept it," undoubtedly promotes discussion. For what it's worth, I don't consider this sentence to be an opt-out clause for those not in agreement with Jesus. Taking his teachings as a whole, I can't think of an instance where he endorses disobedience because the hearer doesn't like what is being said! I read the final sentence as being akin to, "Those who have ears, let them hear," often cited elsewhere in the Scriptures. I leave you to come to your own conclusions.

The End Of The Story?

Anyone who sneeringly declares that to choose Christianity is to take the soft option in life clearly has never taken the plunge! There are huge ramifications in choosing to renounce homosexual relationships in deference to one's Christian commitment, and while the blessings are many and varied, the cost of discipleship is high and not everybody lasts the distance.

There are real issues to address if we are to dwell peacefully in the land of blessing. The next chapter, "Living With Loss", offers some thoughts to encourage you in your continuing journey. I finish with a quote from an American feminist, Virginia Postrel, writing in *Reason* magazine (October 1998): "Religious conviction can affect the trade-offs people make in their lives, including trade-offs outsiders find hard to fathom. The histories of religious martyrs are full of such trade-offs. If you think celibacy is tough, try being burned at the stake."

Chapter Thirteen

Living With Loss

"Every time a believer struggles with sorrow or loneliness or ill health or pain and chooses to trust and serve God anyhow, a bell rings out across heaven and the angels give a great shout. Why? Because one more pilgrim has shown that he or she understands that Jesus is worth it all."[34]

Unrealised Dreams

No one is immune from experiencing a sense of loss. It comes in all shapes and sizes: the exam grades that are not quite high enough, the perfect partner who cheats on you, the longed-for baby who never materialises, or the debilitating illness that scuppers future retirement plans.

Some pain can be discarded by a mere shrug of the shoulders; other losses seep into the deepest hollow of our soul where, neglected over the years, they putrefy and infect the inmost core of our personhood. As the "infection" spreads, so our ability to hide the pain lessens, and, eventually, if unchecked, the inevitable happens: one word or one action, the merest slight by another, touches the pain and throws us into a spiral of despair, sometimes leaving us incapable of functioning at the most basic level.

Unearthing The Problem

"As soon as I got off the plane and saw you, I knew I didn't want to marry you," David (not his real name) gently shared.

34. Philip Yancey, *Disappointment with God* (Zondervan, Grand Rapids, 1988), page 170.

The beautiful dinner suddenly became tasteless, and each mouthful merely added to the solid weight I felt inside. It wasn't what David had said that had affected me so much – his disclosure was disappointing, although certainly not devastating – but what knocked me back was the exposure of a long-held subconscious belief about myself: *I had been judged and found wanting.*

David and I had really got on well when we had met a year previously. He lived in the States, and so our friendship grew through phone calls and letters over the subsequent year. Through mutual friends I was able to form a greater understanding of the man, and what I heard was very positive and attractive. I was certainly encouraged to explore the relationship further. Phone calls became weekly and, having met again in the States, we agreed that he would visit England at the end of the summer.

Ignorant of the feelings of devastation that lay ahead, I planned a week suited to both our interests: three visits to the theatre at Stratford-upon-Avon, tours around historical sites and some visits to National Trust gardens. David was lovely company, we were never short of conversation, and on that level at least the visit was fine.

Alone again after he had returned to the States, and trying to ignore the heaviness within, I attempted to continue my work as before. Only by now, the poison of long-held rejection had coursed its way through my body as if carried in the bloodstream. The low-grade depression that had been rumbling in the background over the past few months erupted with devastating consequences. In my mind I was unacceptable, uncared for and unsought. Life had become pointless.

So Much To Lose

"The losses that settle themselves deeply in our hearts and minds are the loss of intimacy through separations, the loss of safety through violence, the loss of innocence through abuse, the loss of friends through betrayal, the loss of love through abandonment, the loss of home through war, the loss of well-being through hunger, heat, and cold, the loss of children through illness or accidents... "[35]

Our role in life, our dignity, and our sense of worth can be ripped from us in an instant, leaving, despite the lack of external marks, only physical pain as an inadequate distraction. We can labour under a sense of injustice as the guilty apparently walk free, and the burden of guilt, whether real or imagined, can cause us to stoop and avoid the gaze even of a loved one. Our identity becomes confused at best or completely lost in the seemingly unending folds of pain. Clinging to reality by the barest fingertips is exhausting and, deprived of sleep and often food, one finally succumbs to the inescapable sense of aloneness without and loneliness within.

In choosing to reject any sexual expression of our homosexual inclination, we may have to face a number of losses. Some will be specific to your life, and other losses will be common to many. Remaining single in the USA usually means that you end up in a shared household of some description. Remaining single in the UK, however, often means living alone. Childlessness can be another loss to face, bringing to the surface a gamut of internal responses. In my 20s and 30s I failed to discover an atom of maternal feeling within, and babies and toddlers could come and go without a hint of broodiness on my part. Now, in my 40s and approach-

---

35. Henri J M Nouwen, *With Burning Hearts* (Orbis Books, Maryknoll, NY, 1994), page 25.

ing the end of my child-bearing potential, I find myself noticing and caring about the young.

Living alone and child-free in a non-tactile country like England promotes near-insatiable feelings of skin hunger. Watching families in a park, for instance, as they play rough-and-tumble or lie around soaking up one another's company in the warm sunshine, can produce a deep sense of being "apart" and may plant seeds of resentment and bitterness if left unchecked.

How do we address the sense of loss we may be experiencing? Is there an answer? What does God say on the matter?

The Big Vision

When we feel trapped in a cavern of darkness, it is impossible to see anything in the immediate vicinity, let alone focus on the big picture!

The grumbling depression finally took hold of me in early 1995. My short-term memory was severely impaired and I was unable to think clearly, let alone read my Bible. Despite this handicap, my faith in and relationship with God remained. It wasn't vibrant and it certainly wasn't vocal, but there was an internal "knowing" within that I was securely held in his everlasting arms (Deuteronomy 33:27a).

Scriptures I had learned over the years came to me as I sat in the hospital garden, and Bible stories and characters kept me company during those long, dark, wakeful nights. All that I had feasted upon during the good times now came back to feed me during my time of need. The Bible exhorts us to "seek the Lord while he may be found" (Isaiah 55:6), and during the early months of my illness I came to appreciate the benefit of such investment. Times of personal shaking do indeed test the faith we claim to possess.

Steps To Take

Recognise the season

Just as it is incongruous to venture outside in shorts and T-shirt when there is snow on the ground and a wind-chill factor of −7°C, it is absurd to put on a mask of delirious joy when your very being is crumbling within. I am reminded of the joke:

> *Question:* How do you wake up with a smile on your face?
> *Answer:* Go to bed with a coat hanger in your mouth.

I know the joke is daft, but there are many women who live with a religious coat hanger in their mouths, claiming victory and joy at every turn while ignoring the inner turmoil. Concealing our response to loss will never promote spiritual growth. The book of Ecclesiastes is very clear: "There is a time for *everything*, and a season for *every* activity under heaven" (Ecclesiastes 3:1, emphasis mine).

I know that people can turn and quote me reams of Scripture, all based on joy. Indeed "the joy of the Lord *is* my strength" (Nehemiah 8:10b), and that is how I was able to walk through, and not drown in, my illness. Real joy is found when we allow Jesus to expose and touch and heal that hurting part of us. As God's Holy Spirit uncovers the various losses we have felt, we can legitimately grieve over each loss, knowing that he will accompany us on the journey from exposure through to healing.

I need to mourn the likelihood that I will never feel emotionally equipped to marry, and I need to mourn the certainty that I shall never know what it's like to carry a child for nine months, or be a mother, or delight in the status of grandmother. As those feelings are given permission to surface, I need to confess any anger or resentment I have harboured against God.

Use Scripture wisely

"Which of you, if his son asks for bread, will give him a stone? Or if he asks for a fish, will give him a snake? If you, then, though you are evil, know how to give good gifts to your children, how much more will your Father in heaven give good gifts to those who ask him!" (Matthew 7:9–11).

Have you asked God for the equivalent of bread or fish? Do you feel as though you have been given a stone and a snake? How long have you prayed the same prayers regarding a change in your orientation, or recovery from the effects of abuse, or developing a sense of belonging? Have you prayed the same prayer over the past weeks and months, or even over the course of years? Do you look around and see God answering the prayers of others and consider yourself overlooked? Does life seem unfair?

When our hopes, plans and expectations fail to materialise, we have a choice. We can sulk or rage against God because the "good gifts" he promised have never materialised and, in frustration and anger, hurl Scripture back at God, accusing him of not keeping his part of the bargain. Or we can trust that God knows the gifts that will *truly* bless us. It's not that he has given us a stone or a snake, it's just that he hasn't, at least yet, given us the granary loaf and the fresh-water salmon we think we need.

In the pain of our loss, we choose either to reject God and his ways, or to be transformed by the experience. Jesus asked for the cup of suffering to be taken away from him. It wasn't. Paul asked three times for the thorn in his side to be removed. It wasn't. In his obedience Jesus became the Saviour of the world, and Paul's acceptance of his thorn enabled him to grow in grace and humility, thus enabling God's power to work more freely through him. In the anguish of our loss, let us not use Scripture as a weapon of war against God, but as a source of encouragement and hope for ourselves as we continue to seek God's perspective and will.

Change the question

Why me? Why was I a victim of abuse? Why don't I fit in? Why am I still attracted to women? Why haven't I found a husband? Why won't God let me have children?

The questions are endless and, I have to say, for the most part, unanswerable. We have to move on. I can waste a lifetime fathoming the reasons why my natural inclinations are to invest in a lesbian relationship, or to dissect the reasons why I can't relate to a man any further than on the level of friendship. But in so doing, am I missing the point? Surely the Christian response to happenings is not to labour under the "whys" but to love and commit to the Lord with our whole heart, body and soul.

I can't help but agree with Jeanne Guyon, whom Philip Yancey quotes in his book *Reaching for the Invisible God*:[36] "If knowing answers to life's questions is absolutely necessary to you, then forget the journey. You will never make it, for this is a journey of unknowables, of unanswered questions, enigmas, incomprehensibles, and most of all, things unfair." Once we can get beyond the question *Why?* and accept the *Why not?* we can begin to explore the *What now?* question which places us firmly within earshot of God's whispering voice.

---

36. Philip Yancy, *Reaching for the Invisible God* (Zondervan, Grand Rapids, 2000), page 61.

Be reconciled to God

"The secret things belong to the Lord our God, but the things revealed belong to us and to our children for ever, that we may follow all the words of this law" (Deuteronomy 29:29).

Let us not demand to see, know and understand all things before we trust in God's plan for us. What is faith, but to walk in the twilight of the unknown, seeing just far enough ahead to follow our Lord?

And where will following Jesus take us? To the cross. As we nail our hopes, plans, desires and dreams to the cross, we are free to follow the plans he has for us. I offer God my strengths and weaknesses, my gifts and my foibles, my trust and my fears, so that he can transform them.

"In a large house there are articles not only of gold and silver, but also of wood and clay; some are for noble purposes and some for ignoble. If a man cleanses himself from the latter, he will be an instrument for noble purposes, made holy, useful to the Master and prepared to do any good work" (2 Timothy 2:20f). I want to be used for noble purposes. I want to be useful to the Master, and I want to have surrendered my life sufficiently so that I am prepared to do "any good work". Is that what you want? If we can spend our energy on God's present and future plans for us, based on who we are rather than on who we would like to be, then the talents will be invested wisely, rather than kept in our pockets until we feel better equipped to use them.

You may want a husband, 1.8 children, a four-bedroom house and a Range Rover parked in the driveway, but your heavenly Father *may have other plans*. To yield and submit to him is to begin living, not out of a sense of loss, but out of the possibility of what might be.

Trust in God's power

"I want to know Christ and the power of his resurrection, and the fellowship of sharing in his sufferings" (Philippians 3:10a). Suffering without Christ appears meaningless and often leads to despair. The order of Paul's statement is no accident. We need to know the power available if we are to face the fellowship of Christ's suffering with any confidence. And what is this fellowship? As we deny ourselves the option of self-determination for the sake of the gospel, we share in Christ's suffering. Jesus humbled himself, became a man and was obedient even unto death. As we follow in Christ's footsteps, we too must walk the path of humble obedience.

To know the truth of Easter Sunday morning encourages us to endure our own Good Friday as we die to self for the sake of future joy. Some situations in life are resolved over time and we can indulge and delight in joy today. Other situations are long-term, and we may have to live in the uncertainty of Easter Saturday for the duration of this life. But we can remain faithful to the call, knowing that we will experience the joy and release of Easter Sunday when we are finally united with Christ in heaven.

Stop snatching, start giving

"The New Testament persistently presses us upward, toward higher motives for being good. A child wants to know what she can get away with; an adult understands that boundaries exist for his own good; a parent voluntarily sacrifices her freedom for the sake of others."[37]

As stated earlier in the chapter, the book of Ecclesiastes encourages us to recognise the legitimacy of different seasons in our lives. To move on to the next stage can be extremely

---

37. Philip Yancey, *Reaching for the Invisible God* (Zondervan, Grand Rapids, 2000), page 237.

hard. Firstly, there is a certain security in the familiarity of our situation, no matter how painful that may be. Change is uncertain and can engender much fear, but a change of season must occur if we are to grow in God. Secondly, to move on from a state of loss can almost feel like a betrayal of that object of loss, be that your innocence, a person, or, perhaps, your long-held lesbian identity.

When Satan approached Eve in the Garden of Eden, he didn't engage her in conversation about her perfect relationship with God or direct her thoughts towards the numerous blessings at her fingertips, but he made the one thing forbidden to Eve, the tree of the knowledge of good and evil, her focal point.

If we don't move on from our object of loss, then we, like Eve, will ultimately focus on the one tree we can't eat from, rather than delight in all the colours, fragrances and sounds available to us in the garden. Our relationship with God will be stunted, and we will mark time in our Christian walk.

Maturing in Christ requires an ever-broadening vision that compels us to meet other people's needs rather than seek our own comfort, to serve rather than be served, and to know that, as we daily pick up our cross, we are walking in the footsteps of our Lord.

Moving From Loss To Life

A recovering alcoholic does not spend every night in the pub, testing his commitment to give up drinking. Similarly, if you are committed to living a celibate life for the sake of the kingdom, it would be wise to spend time with those who endorse your decision. Seek out those in your fellowship, single, married, male and female, who will encourage you and be encouraged by you in the pursuit of holiness.

Foster intimacy in your relationships. Obviously, this takes time and depends on the cooperation of others, but as a group of you mutually share time, hopes, thoughts and ideas with each other, a sense of natural closeness occurs which can meet some of your real need to know and be known by others.

Learning godly contentment is a lifetime commitment. Ill health, redundancy, relocation and increased age all challenge our contented state, to say nothing of the internal issues we may still have to address. Learning godly contentment is an "everybody" problem, and friends can help carve a path through the minefield of possible difficulties. When discontent arises it may be helpful to ask, *Where is God in this change? Have I placed him or the issue in the centre of my life?*

If you want to spend time with other singles in the church, fine, but don't feel pressurised, especially in a small church, to make this happen. Just because people are single doesn't mean that they have anything else in common with you! Church leadership can often "deal" with the issue of singleness in the church by lumping all singles together and calling it a ministry!

How much time and emotional effort should you invest in pursuing a human relationship? To say that I had a tendency towards obsession would not be overstating the case, and that pattern didn't stop when I moved away from homosexual relationships. After a few years of emotional celibacy, and when I still lived under the belief that I would seamlessly move on from being attracted to my own gender towards an attraction to men, much time was spent wondering where he would come from, what he would do, what he would look like, and whether he would be a strong enough Christian.

The last three years have been gloriously freeing. Having removed that great weight of needing to "feel heterosexual" and perhaps be attracted to a man, I have been able to put my time and emotions into my relationship with God. In so doing, he has enabled me to be myself and *feel all right about it*.

Falling in love and experiencing the peaks and valleys of a relationship is certainly invigorating and keeps the pulse racing. When those relationships are absent it is easy to feel that you've flat-lined; life takes on a grey and rather "blah" quality. Left unchecked, one may be encouraged to seek thrills and spills in all the wrong places. May I encourage you to hurl yourself out of a plane (preferably with a parachute!), go white-water rafting, learn to surf, ride the biggest roller coasters, or engage in the occasional activity that will keep the blood whizzing around the body. Your adrenal glands need the exercise!

Keep Going

Satan will want to use any sense of loss as a weapon against us, our commitment to God, and our part in furthering the kingdom. Learning to live with certain losses that cannot be fully resolved requires a maturity that can develop only as we submerge our roots further into our relationship with Jesus. If you have been sinking rather than swimming, marking time rather than marching forward, or glancing back at Egypt rather than gazing into the face of your Saviour, then take this opportunity to recommit to our Lord and continue your journey of faith. The Hebrews "ranged from rejoicing to mourning, from triumph to trials, from celebrating to complaining, from the mountaintops to darkest valleys, from mighty deliverances to disgraceful defeats, from the sublime to the ridiculous. And God never failed them."[38]

---

38. Philip Mohabir, *Pioneers or Settlers?* (Scripture Union, Milton Keynes, 1991), page 65.

There is another area of loss many labour under because it is so fundamental to life: touch. Studies have shown that at eight weeks old, when the embryo is less than an inch long and has neither eyes nor ears, the baby will respond to touch on its upper lip or nose. The earlier a function develops *in utero*, the more fundamental it is likely to be. Touch is not only the first sense to develop, it is also the last sense to go at the point of death. Is it any wonder that many Christian singles, starving for touch, tired of their vain search to legitimately satisfy their skin hunger, ultimately yield to sin?

What can we do to address this fundamental issue?

Chapter Fourteen

Redeeming Touch: Suitable, Safe And Satisfying

"Why are we so limited in our touching? The answer is social consciousness. Our society inhibits expressions of love, and, as a result, touching behaviour. How sad for us. How sad for the millions of human beings who would give anything to have what one person's beloved cat or dog gets in the loving and touching department – even for one day. How ironic that animals in our society receive what we, as human beings, need so much."[39]

Time To Emigrate?

Thoughts of emigration crossed my mind when I first read the results of a study on touch. In 1966, Jourard, a renowned humanistic psychologist, observed pairs of people sitting in cafés in San Juan (Puerto Rico), Paris, Gainesville (Florida), and London. Counting the number of times that one person made physical contact with the other during a one-hour time period, Jourard was able to show differences in cultural behaviour regarding touch.

People in San Juan proved to be the most tactile, scoring a very satisfactory 180, equivalent to one instance of physical contact for every 20 seconds of conversation. What bliss! The Parisians scored 110, averaging nearly two touches per

---

39. Phyllis K Davis, *The Power of Touch* (Hay House, Carlsbad, CA, 1991), page 1.

minute, whereas those of Anglo-Saxon origin appeared devoid of most forms of contact. At least in Florida, the observed couple managed a score of two, whereas it appears the coffee-drinkers in London failed to register a mark on the chart! They didn't even indulge in a perfunctory handshake!

An Island Race

Would the experiment, 40 years on, uncover a different result? I'd venture to say that the situation regarding touch deprivation in the UK has worsened, and I've no reason to believe it has improved anywhere else in the world.

Much has changed since the 1960s. According to the 2001 UK census, 30 per cent of all households are now single-person occupancy.[40] Private rather than public means of transport dominate personal travel, and improved technology means that, thanks to the Internet, I can contact more people than those of an earlier generation without ever having to meet any of them! Online banking and shopping from the privacy of my house mean I need never face the bank manager or grace a supermarket or clothes shop ever again. Working from home eliminates the grind of a busy commute and the need to be pleasant to colleagues, or to suffer the boredom of an office party. With the God Channel on TV, a proliferation of Christian radio shows, books and worship music to order, unless I *make* myself leave the house, I can live like a modern-day Robinson Crusoe and not meet another person for days at a time!

Changes in educational practice now mean that physical contact between teacher and pupil has all but disappeared for fear of misinterpretation of intent. Parental work commit-

---

40. www.statistics.gov.uk.

ments, along with a divided home life due to increased separation and divorce, mean that many children receive less contact time (literally) with their parents than ever before.

On film and television and in the media, the expressions of touch appear to jump from zero to sexual, leaping over all points in between. Fear of lawsuits claiming sexual harassment or abuse prevails, driving an increasing wedge between individuals. Despite what the poet John Donne may say, each man, woman and child has indeed become an island[41] in the 21st century. Operating in a permanent state of apology, we British navigate our way along busy streets, muttering "Sorry" when others accidentally touch our arm or shoulder in passing.

An Unfavourable Outlook

Norman Autton writes,

> Throughout adult life physical contact appears to be severely restricted. Argyle (1975) lists a number of socially defined circumstances where such contact is acknowledged as permissible: (a) with one's spouse, both during sexual activity and in the more casual circumstances of everyday domestic life; (b) with children, up to adolescence; (c) with other relations and friends in various kinds of greetings and farewells, including handshakes and embraces; and (d) between relative strangers, and in public places, bodily contact is rare.[42]

---

41. John Donne, "Devotions Upon Emergent Occasions, Meditation XVII": "No man is an island, entire of itself... any man's death diminishes me, because I am involved in mankind; and therefore never send to know for whom the bell tolls; it tolls for thee."

42. Norman Autton, *Touch* (Darton, Longman and Todd, London, 1989), page 36.

For those who are not married and have no children, and no close relationships with family members, a severe deficit of permissible touch may exist.

This touch deprivation has worrying social implications. Feelings of isolation and loneliness can result in a spiralling retreat from social activities and all but the most basic inter-action with others. However, recent studies also show that a deprivation of touch can also cause frustration, resulting in more hostile behaviour and, ultimately, violence. Violence is not only focused externally. Montagu writes, "Unexpressed feelings of frustration, rage, and guilt, as well as the strong repressed need for love, may find symptomatic expression in the form of scratching even in the absence of itching. Scratching may be simultaneously a source of pleasure and of displeasure, expressing guilt and a tendency towards self-punishment. Disturbances in sexuality and hostility are almost always present in patients with pruritis."[43] [See foot-note for explanation of pruritis.]

Orphanages

Numerous images of squalid orphanages have been relayed into our living rooms over recent years. Since the fall of Communism, TV cameras have accessed hitherto unknown depths of deprivation in the Eastern Bloc countries, and we know of problems elsewhere in the world such as the many

---

43. Ashley Montagu, *Touching: The Human Significance of the Skin* (Columbia University Press, 1971), pages 154, 155. There are four types of pruritis/itching/scratching: general (like eczema), anal (usually a male condition), female genitalia, chronic (small area such as neck or leg). Often heat-induced, these forms of pruritis can result in recurring sleep disturbance. There is no known cure, but if an underlying disorder is successfully addressed, the pruritis generally ceases to occur.

"orphaned" girls of China and the "children of sin" in Tunisia. Much has been done to alleviate the physical conditions of these children, but, owing to the great emotional needs of each child, there are still major problems to overcome. It is known that touch deprivation denies a child the necessary conditions to thrive, even if other needs such as food and clothing are met. If the children live, life is still not problem-free, for studies have shown physical manifestations of speech retardation and learning disabilities present in many of these youngsters. Incidences of emotional and affective problems such as schizophrenia have also been diagnosed.

Benefits Of Touch

Touch changes people. Even the most loving language retains a gulf between the speaker and the listener, but touch bridges that gap. Good touch affirms a person's sense of being and value; it can lift a mood, promote self-confidence and dampen feelings of anxiety.

Diana, Princess of Wales sent shockwaves around the world back in the early 1980s when a photograph of her holding the hand of an Aids patient was published. Yet that one gesture did much to counteract the false fears held by so many concerning the dangers of catching the HIV virus. *Diana, the future Queen of England, touched an untouchable.* By holding hands with a dying man, Diana helped revolutionise palliative care for Aids patients in this country. She offered rapport, not judgment, interest rather than apathy, and love instead of bigotry.

Questions For Christians

We may feel incapable of alleviating the problems of those overseas, and we certainly don't have the public exposure that Diana once had, but what can we offer within our immediate environment? Do we, as Christians, help or compound the skin hunger experienced by so many people? As a congregation, does our welcome extend no further than a verbal greeting and the "right hand of fellowship"? How do we address the variety of needs that present themselves each week?

On any given Sunday in a local church, there will be individuals coping with touch issues. It may be a young mother releasing a child who no longer needs to be held, or parents feeling alienated from a hostile teenager. There will be incidences in the fellowship of marital intimacy having all but disappeared, or men and women currently dealing with separation or divorce. Someone that week will have experienced the death of a loved one, or been the victim of domestic abuse, while others face the daily grind of living alone. Many people will be coping with old age, and there are always people of any age living with disability.

Time To Get Personal

Perhaps it's time to get more personal. How are you doing regarding the issue of touch? Are you living out of a sense of fullness or deprivation? Does your skin long to feel the tenderness of another skin resting against it? I remember at one stage in my life, out of sheer desperation, purposefully boarding a tube train during the London rush hour. I knew there would be no tenderness of touch, but I needed the jostling and pushing of others to remind me that I still existed.

How do you deal with this sense of physical isolation?

Have you led a "full life" prior to your conversion, or perhaps you had a period of living back in Egypt, and now want to know how to alleviate that longing for meaningful touch without compromising your faith? As we address our own needs, perhaps we can open doors to others within our fellowship, helping them to explore the nuances of touch without fear of sin or fear of rejection.

Suitable Touch

Soppy Labrador puppies hurl themselves at any unsuspecting human being, convinced that they will be loved, accepted and cuddled unceasingly for the next fourteen years! Unfortunately, some humans develop a similar mindset and demolish any touch boundary an individual may have erected. But touch is seen in a positive light only when, by both parties, it is deemed to be appropriate to a given situation. To some, a mere touch on the arm is as intimate as they can get, and some poor women, unable to distinguish between different types of touch, see all contact as being violent. There are women who regard certain parts of their body, like their shoulders or neck, as being completely out of bounds, whereas others see all touch as being appropriate and welcome.

Until an individual discloses his or her boundary of acceptable touch, one must proceed with caution. Our aim must be to promote healing and acceptance and not to reinforce negative and often painful feelings.

Safe Touch

At some time most of us have been the recipients of unsafe touch. It needn't have been dangerous to our health, but it has felt uncomfortable. An individual may have declared a desire to give you a hug, leaving you with a feeling that something has been snatched away rather than given. Safe touch should always leave the recipient feeling complete, cared for, and valued.

In coming from a homosexual inclination, it is important that we are settled in our mind regarding our motivation towards other women. Whereas men are more visually inclined, women are very sensitive to the raft of meaning conveyed through physical contact. We may be verbally saying one thing, but our non-verbal communication can be sending a very different message to the recipient. Touch is not an exact science, and much confusion can result from mixed messages being offered by the giver and then interpreted and even reinterpreted by the recipient. It is imperative that the touch we offer is honouring to the individual and springing from godly motives.

Can The Bible Offer Any Guidance?

Without offering an in-depth study on this subject, we read in the Old Testament that touch played an important part in Hebrew life. All that was deemed holy was not to be touched unless ordained by God, and that included the mountain, Sinai, on which God gave Moses the Law. The Ark of the Covenant and its contents could be touched only by the Levites, and certain foods and women at different times of their life were deemed unclean and, therefore, untouchable.

However, there are incidences when God commands the use of touch: "So the Lord said to Moses, 'Take Joshua son of Nun, a man in whom is the spirit, and lay your hand on him. Make him stand before Eleazar the priest and the entire assembly and commission him in their presence'... Then he laid his hands on him and commissioned him, as the Lord instructed through Moses" (Numbers 27:18, 19, 23). The lay-ing-on of hands was routinely used as a means to bless children and other family members. Touch was also used during healing, although the prophet Elijah dispensed with the mere use of the hands and stretched out his body upon the widow's son during prayer, thus bringing him back from the dead (1 Kings 17:21, 22a). On the Day of Atonement, one goat was offered up in sacrifice while the high priest laid his hands on the head of another goat, symbolically transferring the sins of the people onto the animal. The goat was then led out into the wilderness, thus cleansing the Jews from all their sins.

The New Testament continues the theme of blessing, healing and commissioning incorporating the use of touch. However, the main difference between the two testaments is evident when one considers Jesus. God the Untouchable of the Old Testament becomes God Incarnate, the one who invites touch.

The little children eagerly came to Jesus for blessing (Mark 10:13). John the apostle leaned against his Master's chest during dinner, and Jesus commended Mary Magdalene for her act of worship in wiping his feet with her hair.

Throughout his ministry, crowds followed Jesus, all hoping to touch him and receive healing (Mark 3:10, Luke 6:19). His power and authority were such that the desperate multitudes knew that if they just touched his garments, healing would occur (Matthew 9:20ff, Matthew 14:35b–36). God had become accessible to all through Jesus.

Jesus not only welcomed touch, he offered it too. Some examples follow:

"They came to Bethsaida, and some people brought a blind man and begged Jesus to touch him. He took the blind man by the hand and led him outside the village. When he had spat on the man's eyes and put his hands on him, Jesus asked,

'Do you see anything?' He looked up and said, 'I see people; they look like trees walking around.' Once more Jesus put his hands on the man's eyes. Then his eyes were opened, his sight was restored, and he saw everything clearly" (Mark 8:22ff).

"He touched her hand and the fever left her, and she got up and began to wait on him" (Matthew 8:15).

"Jesus had compassion on them and touched their eyes. Immediately they received their sight and followed him" (Matthew 20:34).

And just as Diana, Princess of Wales didn't merely "brush" but *held* the hand of the Aids patient, Jesus held (*hapto* – Greek: "fastened to") the leper: "Jesus reached out his hand and touched [*hapto*] the man. 'I am willing,' he said. 'Be clean!' Immediately he was cured [made clean] of his leprosy" (Matthew 8:3).

Jesus also used physical touch to allay fear: "When the disciples heard this, they fell face down to the ground, terrified. But Jesus came and touched them. 'Get up,' he said. 'Don't be afraid.' When they looked up, they saw no one except Jesus" (Matthew 17:6–8).

What Can We Do?

Considering the social and religious restrictions of the day, Jesus offered and received remarkable physical contact from men, women and children alike. He obviously presented as a non-threatening man of immense integrity for such a broad range of needy people to be so vulnerable in his company. Is it possible for us to reflect that security to those we meet and spend time with?

Much will depend on how much love we ourselves are able to receive and retain. As mentioned in the chapter "Coronary Care", a heart that is itself in need will have little to offer.

Dealing with much of our pain, damage and sense of loss is imperative before life-giving love can be offered in any great measure. Failure to remain within this order promotes the possible development of unhealthy relationships. We also need to receive good healthy touch, although leaping on unsuspecting strangers, demanding a hug, is not to be encouraged. While a goldfish is rather limited in its ability to offer affection, pets in general are an excellent source of touch therapy. While I accept that they do not fulfil all of life's desires and needs, animals can remove the sharp edge of need at the most opportune times. A word of warning: choose your pet carefully. Caleb, my ginger cat, is fickle to say the least, offering the most disdainful of stares if I dare to approach without an invite. One has to be strong in the first place to withstand the repeated rejection he volunteers! Indoor litter-trained rabbits just love being stroked and cuddled, and the more one handles rats the more affectionate they become. Borrowing a friend's dog if you are unable to have your own also helps meet many touch needs.

What About Humans?

Booking yourself a monthly massage or facial can be very therapeutic. If you are young and fit enough, joining a club offering contact sport such as women's rugby may give you more than your fair share of touch!

Toddlers are tactile. Having lived with one for a year, I know how much we both benefited from safe, uninhibited touch. Not only were there the rough-and-tumble times, there were also the cuddling and holding moments, and the times when he needed me for security and food. I encourage you to consider investing in a family with young children, as the blessing really can be mutual. And remember, you get to give them back to the parents at the grouchy time of the day!

In your fellowship, too, you may want to offer time in the children's work. Once the mandatory police checks have been cleared, there can be much to do. Perhaps it is a chance to demonstrate affirming touch, help offset damaging touch that may have occurred elsewhere, and minister to those already experiencing touch deprivation.

Noting the need for sensitivity mentioned earlier in the chapter, there are many potential recipients for meaningful touch present in any gathering of people: the singles, the elderly and the infirm, to name but three. I find the leadership in my church are always up for a hug, irrespective of age, gender or marital status. The more we can retain of God's love, the more we will be able to offer to others, and because we are not exuding an air of overwhelming neediness, we will find that many seek to offer us a "right hug of fellowship".

Communicating God's Love

Worldly love and touch often come with a hefty price tag: trade-offs, such as sexual intercourse for a sense of belonging, occur in all walks of life. In contrast, the best love we can offer is that which is unconditional, life-enhancing, and touched by the Holy Spirit. "Touch is essentially the sign and sense of love par excellence, and in order to find the profound meaning of touch we must see it from the point of view of love. When an outward and human touch becomes transformed by an inward and divine love, it is then, and then only, that we are able to bring solace to the sad, strength to the weak and healing to the sick."[44]

I don't pretend to have all the answers on this very

---

44. Norman Autton, *Touch* (Darton, Longman and Todd, London, 1989), page 141.

important subject, but I do know that the topic cannot be ignored. Like the poor orphans in many countries, humans from every walk of life can be well fed, clothed and educated, and still fail to thrive due to the lack of meaningful touch. Unlike those poor orphans, however, we can do something about it. I appreciate that you may be of the view that nothing comes close to the satisfaction of the skin-on-skin touch of a loved one; however, if we have closed the door to that expression outside the boundaries of heterosexual marriage, then we must find meaningful tactile expression elsewhere. Ignoring this need, I fear, will make us susceptible to the wiles of Satan, but godly, creative exploration may highlight some of those numbers between zero and sexual. It is a tough call, seeking to redeem touch when it would be very easy to think and behave as the world does, but may I encourage you, as a pilgrim, to keep the goal of your journey in mind. At journey's end we will fall into our Father's welcoming and all-satisfying hug that will last for the whole of eternity.

Joshua entered the Promised Land knowing that God had given it to his people. He also knew that claiming the land would not come without a fight, but through the victories and defeats, the blessing and the disciplining, Joshua matured in his relationship with God. In the final chapter, let us explore three characteristics that will enable us not only to live, but to dwell in the land.

Chapter Fifteen

Faith, Hope And Love

"But, as great as all this was, my sexual orientation did not change; I still was not then, nor am I now, 'normal'. And that's what I wish I could be: normal. I've tried to change, tried to become heterosexual, tried just about everything to do so! Counseling, therapy, prayer, healing – you name it. But for all my trying, all I've managed to do is control the behavioural manifestations of my sexual orientation. God has given me the power to live a fulfilling heterosexual life [the author is married with children], together with the grace to live with the fact that I'm still homosexual. It hasn't been an easy victory. There are times when maintaining this dichotomous life is nearly overwhelming."[45]

Congregational president, youth group leader, athletics coach, husband and father – these are the credentials of the author of the above quote. He wrote anonymously for fear that his Christian friends and co-leaders would strip him of his leadership position and reject him as a person if they knew of his near-daily struggle with homosexuality: "Perhaps I'm hypersensitive in not trusting, but I've overheard too many jokes, seen too many expressions of hate directed at homosexuals, to believe that these same people could be my friends if they knew."[46]

What a sad indictment of the church today.

---

45. Anonymous, "No Easy Victory", *Christianity Today* magazine, 11 March 2002, Vol. 46, No. 3, page 50.
46. Ibid.

The Call To Persevere

Leaving aside the response of society in general, it appears that the homosexual issue will continue to unsettle the Christian church in the foreseeable future. What of the individual? How are you going to remain true to God's teaching while those around succumb to liberal pressure and dilute God's call to celibacy outside the realm of heterosexual marriage? How are you going to remain true to yourself while an unyielding right wing overlooks mercy and grace in their pursuit of righteousness? Do you live, like the poor brother in the above quote, faithfully serving God and yet fearful of God's people?

"Blessed is the [woman] who perseveres under trial, because when [she] has stood the test, [she] will receive the crown of life that God has promised to those who love him" (James 1:12). But fearing the response of God's people should not be one of the trials we persevere under. I long for an open and transparent church where we not only welcome the sinner from afar, but also embrace him or her as one of "us". I long to hear admissions of perseverance under difficulty, grace through temptation, and restoration after failure from those in leadership so that we, the average churchgoer, can empathise and be encouraged in our own pilgrimage. No one wants a leader seemingly so far along the path that he or she is a mere speck in the distance, unconnected with the body. I think of those movies depicting the journeys that early settlers in the 19th century made across the United States. They followed one another in horse-drawn wagons, unsure of what was ahead and fearful of the dangers on the way. The leader not only posted armed riders at intervals along the wagon train, but he himself would often ride back along the line, personally checking on the weary travellers and encouraging them in their journey.

May I commend you in your journey of faith, hope, and love.

Five Kings And One Wise Man

"The most fearful sight to the camp of the Enemy is the Word of God in the hands of a humble man who will not compromise his convictions."[47]

Obedience always provokes opposition. Faith is costly but it is also powerful, as we read in the tenth chapter of Joshua. The Hebrews had learned that relying on their own assessment and understanding brought shame, defeat and death, but that responding to God's ways always brought victory. After their ill-judged pact with the Gibeonites, Joshua took his people back to God's presence at Gilgal.

> Why do the nations rage
> and the peoples plot in vain?
> The kings of the earth take their stand
> and the rulers gather together against the Lord
> and against his Anointed One.   (Psalm 2:1f)

Throughout the ages, opposition to God has promoted unholy alliances. Principles and ethics that separate various factions are often laid aside in deference to a common stance against God's righteousness. In this instance, five Amorite kings banded together and attacked Gibeon. "So Joshua marched up from Gilgal with his entire army, including all the best fighting men. The Lord said to Joshua, 'Do not be afraid of them; I have given them into your hand. Not one of them will be able to withstand you.' After an all-night march from Gilgal,

---

47. Rick Joyner, *The Journey Begins* (Whitaker House, New Kensington, PA, 1997), page 126.

Joshua took them by surprise. The Lord threw them into confusion before Israel, who defeated them in a great victory at Gibeon" (Joshua 10:7–10a).

The Israelites, without grumbling, marched through the night and routed the combined armies of the enemy. Despite being outnumbered and ill-equipped, the Israelite army trusted in God's promise of victory. Active faith produces greater faith-filled action and we quickly read about the conquest of the cities as far south as Debir and as far north as Sidon.

What a difference faith makes! So much had changed in attitude and belief that when they were faced with the Anakites, the giants who had thwarted the plans of their fathers 40 years earlier, the Israelite army had no trouble conquering them. Victories do not occur along a well-defined time line. Problems that appear insurmountable at one stage in our life can later appear mere trifles, thanks to God's intervention and grace.

Have you experienced long waits in your life? Have you considered making alternative arrangements? Please note the lesson that Joshua had learned. After experiencing amazing victory at Jericho, humiliation and defeat at Ai, and embarrassment at Gibeon, Joshua realised his need to wait in God's presence at Gilgal. He knew what to do: conquer the land and settle the people, but he needed to know *how* to accomplish the task. I don't know the length of waiting time required as we address various issues in our lives, but I do know that in staying close to God we are more likely to hear what he is saying. It may be a word of encouragement as we wait, or a plan he is considering implementing. He may offer us a choice of action, or just whisper sweet words of love to our receptive heart.

Faith requires patience in the waiting and courage in the

implementation. Active faith is costly: "Some faced jeers and flogging, while still others were chained and put in prison. They were stoned; they were sawn in two; they were put to death by the sword. They went about in sheepskins and goatskins, destitute, persecuted and ill-treated – the world was not worthy of them. They wandered in deserts and mountains, and in caves and holes in the ground. These were all commended for their faith" (Hebrews 11:36–39a).

Whatever discomfort we may experience in taking our stand as those not free from homosexual attractions yet refusing to act upon those attractions, let us be encouraged by the faithful witnesses who have gone before and suffered unimaginable hardship and death for their faithfulness. "Let us hold unswervingly to the hope we profess, for he who promised is faithful" (Hebrews 10:23).

Hope For All

"Therefore, strengthen your feeble arms and weak knees! 'Make level paths for your feet,' so that the lame may not be disabled, but rather healed" (Hebrews 12:12).

The son of a yak-herder in Tibet who had never been to school and could neither read nor write, Sherpa Tenzing became a household name on 29 May 1953. Along with the New Zealander Edmund Hillary, this hitherto unknown man became the first person to reach the summit of Mount Everest.

In fact, although Sherpa Tenzing was unknown to the outside world, he was well known within the climbing fraternity as a man whose knowledge of the Himalayas was to be trusted. He had been employed by Western climbers on several expeditions prior to the 1953 climb of Everest and was seen as a reliable guide.

Tenzing Norgay (his real name) subsequently trained generations of Indian mountaineers at the Himalayan Mountaineering Institute in Darjeeling and created work for thousands of people living in the Khumbu region, thereby alleviating the abject poverty of the indigenous population. Although never a Sherpa himself, Tenzing Norgay successfully branded the name, ensuring that his standard of mountain training was maintained and respected throughout the world. Fifty years later, thousands of people literally owe their lives either directly or indirectly to the knowledge and skill of Tenzing Norgay.

How did he become so skilled in his climbing and so trusted by others? He kept himself fit by climbing the foothills, he marked out paths for the higher climbs, and, through continued observation, he learned to read the weather changes throughout the region. He knew his limitations and those of the people he was guiding, and, although engaged in a risk-taking business, he never acted without due consideration or respect for the hostile environment in which he lived. Is it possible that we can view our lives as something akin to a Tibetan Sherpa?

A faith-filled walk speaks volumes to believers and nonbelievers alike. Just as we derive encouragement from Christians who have gone before us, our faithfulness can be a sign of hope to others. As we exercise the gift of faith and pursue a life acceptable to Christ's call, we will become a guide to other pilgrims. Transparent in our struggles and bringing the truth of our conviction into everyday life, we can straighten and smooth paths, indeed give wheelchair access so that others, perhaps more broken than we, can also travel along the path of discipleship.

Make no mistake: our Christian walk will not go unnoticed. How we live our lives will influence others, whether we preach from the pulpit every week or make the coffees after the service. Our attitude towards the difficulties and blessings we experience will either disable other Christians or enable them to face their own particular pilgrimage. What a responsibility! Every aspect of a Christian's life will either lead someone to Jesus or cause him or her to turn away. None of us is a mere neutral observer in the cosmic battle occurring all around.

Love

Why is love the greatest of the three Christian characteristics? *Because God is love.* Because of his love, God can be faithful, and because of his love, God can offer us hope. If God, Love, is not the core of our being, the motivator of our actions, and the reason for our perseverance, then we may as well pursue all the pleasures of the world and take no thought for the eternal. It is only love for, and commitment to, someone greater than myself that brings meaning to my faith. "This is love: not that we loved God, but that he loved us and sent his Son as an atoning sacrifice for our sins" (1 John 4:10).

A person in love wants to please the object of his or her love more than anything else in the world. Kings renounce their thrones, executives forsake their careers, and individuals move to the other side of the world because of love. Books, movies and songs are endlessly created to the glory of this often tenuous state. The world has elevated human love to such a dizzy status that to claim, "I couldn't help myself" appears to absolve us from all moral and legal obligations.

This book encourages attitudes and behaviour that fly in the face of the current societal dictate: *If it feels good and doesn't hurt anyone, do it!* Am I just a sad middle-aged woman who has forgotten how to enjoy myself and wants to drag everyone else down to my puritanical level?

Love And Action

"For God so loved the world that he gave his one and only Son" (John 3:16a).

Jesus did not write books, compose songs or produce a screenplay extolling the virtues of love. He restored dignity to a prostitute, held the untouchable and offered forgiveness and salvation to all. He gave that we may receive, he laid down his deity that we may be lifted up, and he died in agony so that we may live in glory. He was broken so that we need not be crushed.

Love has nothing to do with our "right" to express ourself as we see fit. Love is all about yielding to the One who bought us at such a great price.

As we feed the life that has been placed inside, our love for God and his ways will continue to grow and strengthen. Unfortunately, that passion will incur greater trials as we challenge the conformity to the world both inside and outside the church, but it is a call that Jesus has faced along with all his disciples ever since: "Smyrna, on the other hand, was given the most exalted privilege of all – prolonged opposition, imprisonment and death. The Smyrnans loved Christ with a burning, flaming passion. For them there was to be the highest and most glorious reward of all, the reward of those who are utterly, utterly faithful – that of sharing Christ's personal sufferings."[48]

---

48. John White, *Holiness* (Eagle, Trowbridge, 1996), page 189.

Faithful Response Produces Powerful Ministry

This chapter began with one man's faithful struggle against his natural inclination for the sake of the kingdom. We have no idea how many men, women and children he has touched with God's love over the past years or will touch in the years to come. How many will come to faith because of this man's sacrificial life? Only God knows. Did the Ethiopian eunuch mentioned in an earlier chapter ever imagine that his faith would still be bringing people to faith today? Highly unlikely.

I don't know what service God intends for you as his child. But I do know that, as you prove faithful in little, he will entrust you with more. He will also "gift" you with a greater connection in Christ's sufferings so that, in order to go on, you are compelled to know and trust in him with every fibre of your being.

Thankfulness

For many years I longed for a "normal" problem so that I could "get on" and serve God better. What foolishness! My inherent sinfulness, my sexual brokenness and my mental health problems have all provided an opportunity to know and rely on God more fully. We have all seen the pictures of drought-stricken countries where nothing can grow and vultures congregate, waiting for the slow, agonising death of its inhabitants. Continual sunshine offers mere survival rather than abundance of life.

Britain is blessed with changeable weather and, although on a cold, rainy day in February we may long for the first signs of spring, we know that the autumn and winter seasons are necessary for a good harvest.

Similarly, I have learned to live through the autumns and

winters of my life, knowing that they are an important part of the overall growth of Christian character. That knowledge doesn't stop me looking out for those first sprouts of spring growth, but it does create in me a faithful trust so that, even if there are no signs of life today, exposure to light and warmth and a little water will eventually result in abundant life.

My friend Meryl experienced a number of difficulties throughout her life. She died unexpectedly from a brain haemorrhage at the age of 42, but a couple of weeks before her death, she wrote the following poem:

SPRING

Take heart, it will soon be spring;
Winter has been harsh,
cold hard elements, scarring bark,
destroying long established branches.
Stark and naked against the grey sky,
shape is defined and structure refined,
disturbed limbs untwisted.

But soon it will be spring.
Rest and be nourished a while;
restore the resources
bled almost dry during those gruelling months.
Be refreshed and strengthened;
stretch out those roots
deep into nutritious soil.
Draw up goodness and sustenance.

For soon it will be spring.
Then, with face tilted up to the Light
you may display the splendour

for which you were created.
The fresh fragrance of new life.
The planting of the Lord
that he may be glorified.

Meryl Joy Amos, 1995

In Conclusion

> True liberty behaves in a manner that is consistent with God's
> higher purposes for us. We are created in God's image, so a per-
> son who is really free has the ability to respect others and to
> live within the bounds of decency, has a conscience free of guilt
> and condemnation, and has the strength to say no to things she
> knows are wrong and detrimental to her welfare. Freedom is
> the inner strength to follow your own convictions, not to yield
> to the pressures of society or your peers just to keep up with the
> "in crowd", even if it means that you stand out and look odd.[49]

By definition, any Christian walk should look odd to the
world. We are "sojourners", just passing through on our pilgrimage towards a better place. Sometimes that walk will be
a joyous celebration accompanied by fellow pilgrims united
in purpose and expectation. At other times the pilgrimage
will be taken in seeming isolation, buffeted by the elements
and unsure of the hilly path. We will encounter trials and difficulties and there will be challenges to our position from a
variety of sources. But they need not prevail. "These have
come so that your faith – of greater worth than gold, which
perishes even though refined by fire – may be proved genuine
and may result in praise, glory, and honour when Jesus Christ
is revealed" (1 Peter 1:7).

---

49. Philip Mohabir, *Pioneers or Settlers?* (Scripture Union, Milton Keynes,
     1991), page 44.

As you make progress through the Promised Land, you will encounter strongholds and difficulties. There will be people who oppose you and others who tempt you to stray from your determined path. But there will be many fellow pilgrims pursuing a similar holy goal. Let their commitment and determination encourage you in your efforts so that you, too, may encourage those who follow.

"So Joshua took the entire land, just as the Lord had directed Moses, and he gave it as an inheritance to Israel according to their tribal divisions.

Then the land had rest from war" (Joshua 11:23).

Bibliography

Auld, A Graeme, *The Daily Study Bible: Joshua, Judges and Ruth* (Saint Andrew Press, Edinburgh, 1987).

Autton, Norman, *Touch: An Exploration* (Darton, Longman and Todd, London, 1989).

Berry, Carmen Renee, *Your Body Never Lies* (PageMill Press, Berkeley, CA, 1993).

Bickle, Mike, *Passion for Jesus* (Kingsway, Eastbourne, 1994).

Davis, Phyllis K, *The Power of Touch* (Hay House, Carlsbad, CA, 1991).

Frangipane, Francis, *Holiness, Truth and the Presence of God* (Arrow, Cedar Rapids, IA, 1994); UK version: *In the Presence of God* (New Wine Press, Bognor Regis, 1994).

Fyall, Robert, *A Spiritual Pilgrimage* (SPCK, London, 1996).

Hume, Basil, *To Be a Pilgrim* (Triangle, SPCK, London, 1999).

Joyner, Rick, *A Prophetic Vision for the 21st Century* (Thomas Nelson, Nashville, TN, 1999).

Joyner, Rick, *The Journey Begins* (Whitaker House, New Kensington, PA, 1997).

Kendall, R T, *The Thorn in the Flesh* (Hodder and Stoughton, London, 1999).

Mohabir, Philip, *Pioneers or Settlers?* (Scripture Union, Milton Keynes, 1991).

Montagu, Ashley, *Touching: The Human Significance of the Skin* (Columbia University Press, 1971).

Murray, Andrew, *Waiting on God* (Moody Press, chicago, 1990).

Nouwen, Henri J M, *In the House of the Lord* (Darton, Longman and Todd, London, 1994).

Nouwen, Henri J M, *The Inner Voice of Love* (Image, Doubleday, New York, 1998).

Nouwen, Henri J M, *With Burning Hearts* (Orbis Books, Maryknoll, NY, 1994).

Schmidt, Thomas E, *Straight and Narrow? Compassion and Clarity in the Homosexuality Debate* (InterVarsity Press, Downers Grove, IL, 1995).

Stott, John, *New Issues Facing Christians Today* (Marshall Pickering, London, 1999).

White, John, *Holiness: A Guide for Sinners* (Eagle, Trowbridge, 1996).

Yancey, Philip, *Disappointment with God* (Zondervan, Grand Rapids, 1988).

Yancey, Philip, *The Jesus I Never Knew* (Marshall Pickering, London, 1995).

Yancey, Philip, *Reaching for the Invisible God* (Zondervan, Grand Rapids, 2000).

Yancey, Philip, *Where Is God When It Hurts?* (Marshall Pickering, London, 1998).

Regeneration Books is a small non profit ministry that sells Christian books on homosexuality and sexual and relational brokenness. We screen our books to determine that what they teach is consistent with traditional Christianity.

Contact Information:
Regeneration Books
PO Box 9830
Baltimore, MD 21284-9830
Voice 410-661-0284 Fax 410-882-6812
www.regenbooks.org
Email: Regenbooks@regenerationministries.org